Also compiled by John Foster

A Century of Children's Poems

101
FAVOURITE
POEMS

Compiled by John Foster

Illustrated by Clare Mackie
and Tim Stevens

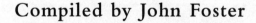

Collins

An imprint of HarperCollins*Publishers*

First published in hardback in Great Britain by Collins in 2002
First published in paperback in Great Britain by Collins in 2003
Collins is an imprint of HarperCollins*Publishers* Ltd,
77–85 Fulham Palace Road, Hammersmith,
London W6 8JB

The HarperCollins website address is:
www.harpercollins.co.uk

1 3 5 7 9 8 6 4 2

This edition copyright © John Foster 2002
Illustrations © Clare Mackie 2002, Tim Stevens 2002
Rhino typography by John Peacock
The acknowledgements on pages 191–192 constitute
an extension of this copyright page.

ISBN 0 00 714438 5

The authors, illustrators and compiler assert the moral right to
be identified as the authors, illustrators and compiler of this work.

Printed and bound in England by
Clays Ltd, St Ives plc

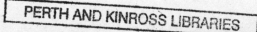

⤚ Contents ⤙

John Agard

One of my favourites, I suppose, because it's about the little things taken for granted and it has a sort of soothing music like a prayer or lullaby.

from Points of View With Professor Peekaboo

Little gaps
in wet stone
that give home
to geranium

Little nooks
and crannies
that shelter
little fungi

Little seeds
of fern
that make an eye
in wonder turn

Little drops
that fall from sky
to polish plants
with dew

Thank you
little things
that enchant
the bigger view.

Allan Ahlberg

I've chosen this poem because the one I would have chosen was too long to fit into this particular anthology. Shame about that. It's a great poem — the longer one, I mean. You would have loved it. Still, never mind, this one's not bad, I suppose… See what you think.

Lost

Dear Mrs Butler, this is just a note
About our Raymond's coat
Which he came home without last night,
So I thought I'd better write.

He was minus his scarf as well, I regret
To say; and his grandma is most upset
As she knitted it and it's pure
Wool. You'll appreciate her feelings, I'm sure.

Also, his swimming towel has gone
Out of his P.E. bag, he says, and one
Of his socks, too — it's purplish and green
With a darn in the heel. His sister Jean

Has a pair very similar. And while
I remember, is there news yet of those fairisle

Gloves which Raymond lost that time
After the visit to the pantomime?

Well, I think that's all. I will close now.
Best wishes, yours sincerely, Maureen Howe
(Mrs). P.S. I did once write before

About his father's hat that Raymond wore

In the school play and later could not find,
But got no reply. Still, never mind,
Raymond tells me now he might have lost the note,
Or left it in the pocket of his coat.

Jez Alborough

I like the way that this poem challenges me, and anyone who reads it aloud, to put on a performance for the listener. A half-hearted reading just won't work. You have to be quite creative in your interpretations of the various coughs.

↬

The Assembly Cough

Cough!

Someone three rows back from me
   coughs in our assembly,
Miss Chadwick squints a beady eye
   and breathes a long and weary sigh.
She knows this sound – she knows the score
   she's heard it many times before
the diagnosis here is plain…
   the *Assembly Cough* has struck again!

Miss Chadwick struts about the place
   and searches for a guilty face
All it takes is just one cough
   to start an epidemic off
She's got the notion in her head
   if stopped at source, this cough won't spread
but before her theory can be tested

Cough!

another cough has manifested.

Miss Chadwick turns around and scowls
　　　　'That's quite enough of that' she growls
We all pretend to concentrate
　　　　on notices from Mrs Tate
but every ear is turned to hear
　　　　from where the next cough will appear
I hope Miss Chadwick doesn't see

　　cough!

I couldn't help it – that was me!

It turns into a free for all
　　　　As coughs spring up around the hall.

COUGH!

　　　Like creatures in the forest calling,

COUGH! COUGH! COUGH! COUGH!

　　　Machine gunfire or engines stalling

COUGH! COUGH! COUGH! COUGH! COUGH!

　　　The epidemic has begun...

COUGH!

　　　I'm sure a teacher did that one!

Miss Chadwick opens up the door
    there's no use fighting any more
COUGH! COUGH!
    This disease has just one cure, she knows:
to bring Assembly to a close.
    As children quietly file outside
COUGH!
    all trace of symptoms soon subside
and once behind the classroom door
    the *Assembly Cough* is heard no more.

This sickness is a teacher's curse
    but Miss Chadwick knows it could be worse
It only takes one child to spawn
    an outbreak of the *Classroom Y - A - W - N !*

Moira Andrew

In Letter from Egypt *I'm trying to let Mary have her say, enabling her to express her own feelings for once. She is usually seen as a shadowy figure in the Nativity story with the kings and shepherds taking centre stage. I like being able to give her the words contemporary women might have used, 'That's men all over! It wouldn't cross their minds to bring a shawl!' That says it all.*

Letter from Egypt

Dear Miriam,
            Just a line
to let you know how things
are with us & of course to
thank you (& your good man)
for all you did for us – &
at your busiest time too
what with the census &
everything. I was quite
exhausted & the baby was
beginning to make himself
felt. If it hadn't been
for your help that night
my baby might have died.

Good of you
to put up with all our
visitors – who'd have
thought, six scruffy
shepherds up & leaving
their sheep like that?
Still they were good-
hearted & they meant well.
I hope they brought some
extra trade to the inn.
They looked in need of
a hot drink & a meal.

& what about
those kings, Miriam? Kneeling
there in their rich robes
& all? & me in nothing but
my old blue dress! Joseph
said not to worry, it was
Jesus they'd come to see.
Real gentlemen *they* were.
But what funny things to
give a baby – gold & myrrh
& frankincense. That's men
all over! It wouldn't cross
their minds to bring a shawl!

Sorry we left
so suddenly. No time for
good-byes with King Herod on
the warpath! We had to take
the long way home & I'm so
tired of looking at sand!
Joseph has picked up a few
jobs mending this & that so
we're managing quite well.
Jesus grows bonnier every
day & thrives on this way
of life, but I can't wait
to see Nazareth again.

Love to all
at the inn,

Mary

Leo Aylen

I grew up in the country, though now I live in the city. But I never want to lose touch with the animals — the magic of night in the country and the scuttling night creatures. I hope I've captured the sense of movement at night, and I've tried to be as accurate as possible about the animals. Hedgehogs do sleep in wasps' nests… what a weird thing to do; one could never invent that!

Greedy Green River

>*Now greedy green river has swallowed the sun,*
>*Timid as twilight, the night creatures come.*

Splodgy scuttlers, reeking of slime,
Darters, and burrowers with luminous eyes,
Scurrying twitterers, swoopers from trees,
With tails that tickle, or scales that gleam,
Or bristles that rustle like wind in dry leaves,

>*Timid as twilight, the night creatures come,*
>*Now greedy green river has swallowed the sun.*

Under the scum on duckweedy ponds
Frogspawn is foaming, tadpoles grow strong.
Toads creep stealthily out of the mud,
Crawl and wobble, and gobble the grubs.
Twigs flutter with moths. Bark oozes with slugs.

Timid as twilight, the night creatures come,
Now greedy green river has swallowed the sun.

Slow-worm wriggles his old bronze skin.
Water-rat plops like a furry fish,
Swimming and nosing his way through the reeds.
Hedgehog sniffs ditches itchy with fleas,
Then curls in a wasp-nest, and falls asleep.

As the sun rises..
Rises..
Rises…

And birds dart out of the branches,
Swooping, wheeling, cackling, and chattering,
Telling the world in a thousand languages:
Look at the light!
Look at the light!
Look at the light!

Gerard Benson

As a boy I used to swim in the River Windrush. I loved writing this poem. It reminded me of that and many other rivers. Although the pattern of the poem is quite complicated it just fell into place; the words seemed to arrive of their own accord. I tried to do two things: to tell the river's story and to give it a voice with a rippling watery rhythm. Once I heard some children reciting it. It was like listening to a small river on a warm summer afternoon. These are some of the reasons why it's my favourite.

Note: the 'rover' in the poem is not a car or a dog but a man who spends his time walking from place to place, a wanderer.

River Song

'Oh where are you going?' said rover to River,
'You flow always downward. Why should that be?'
'I gather the droplets of water together
And carry them home to their mother, the sea.'

'From moment to moment,' said rover to River,
'Your waters are changing, yet you stay the same.'
'No. I am the mocker of every map-maker;
Although they outline me and give me a name.'

'I'm banked and I'm bridged,' said River to rover.
'I'm built by; I'm fished in, I'm wished on as well.
But I am a winder; I love to wander.
Every day I am different, with stories to tell,'

'Of floods and disasters,' said River to rover,
'Of long lazy summers, of ducks in my weeds,
Of wild otter huntings, of strange ghostly hauntings,
Of crisp frozen winters with ice on my reeds.'

'Of towns that surround me,' said River to rover,
'Until I escape through the bridges, to fields
Where brown cattle wallow beside my green willows,
And small beetles strut, with their bright shining shields.'

'And all the time downward,' said River to rover,
'I travel past building and boulder and tree.
I gather the driplets and droplets together
And hurry them home to their mother, the sea.'

James Berry

For me, water has everything that is fantastic and magical. Draped With Water *attempts to celebrate man and water drawn together in an enjoyable unity.*

Draped With Water

See how my diving dip
launches me down and up.

See me take to water
all a water stroker.

Pushing like monster frog
I am no drifter-log.

Silver trail of water
drapes me from the collar.

With my water-dress on
I fly a slow-motion run.

Each face-down movement
brings me fresh contentment.

I feel I fly
between water-depths and sky.

And see I am deeper
in and in with big water.

Then breaking the waves' backs
I ride for the rocks.

Out in a stone recess
I keep my water-caress.

Like a wet seal glistening
I move I flash lightning.

See me sitting tired:
see me happily stirred.

Malorie Blackman

I've chosen I've Done It Again! *because although I first used it in a book I wrote called* Pig-Heart Boy, *I wrote it when I was a teenager and in a moment of great angst! I was told something which, gullible twit that I am, I totally believed when everyone else around me knew it was a load of nonsense. And to make matters worse, I was told it by someone I really fancied. I was so embarrassed I went home and wrote the poem in about a minute and a half, if that! It seemed perfect for Cameron to use when something similar happens to him, hence its inclusion in* Pig-Heart Boy. *I like this poem because it recalls a lot of feelings I had at the time and because it was heart-felt.*

I've Done It Again!

Confidence up, confidence down
Act like an angel, look like a clown,
Changing your mind, changing it back.
The quick recipe for a heart attack.

Smile at your blunders, laugh at my own.
This isn't right, I should be at home.
Under the duvet, safe from attack.
Changing your mind, changing it back.

Accident prone, but never you worry,
I'll tell you when you should leave in a hurry.
Making up ground for the sense that I lack.
Changing your mind, changing it back.

I've done it again; proved my reputation.
Is this sorrow or is it elation?
Statements once given I cannot retract,
Changing your mind, changing it back.

The notice I earn is diluted with patience,
The smiles that I give are the scorns I receive.
While I hold my breath and count to one hundred,
You'll tell me a tale I am sure to believe.

Fanciful feelings hiding a fool,
A cog that's not turning, a bottomless pool.
Lend me what's common, of which you've a stack.
Then I'll change your mind and I won't change it back.

Valerie Bloom

This is one of those poems which present themselves almost as a gift. As soon as I read Thomas Hood's poem November I thought of this and it didn't take long to write it. Poems which come fairly naturally are always a hit with me.

De

inspired by Thomas Hood

De snow, de sleet, de lack o' heat,
De wishy-washy sunlight,
De lip turn blue, de cold, 'ACHOO!'
De runny nose, de frostbite.
De creakin' knee, de misery,
De joint dem all rheumatic,
De icy bed (de blanket dead)
De burs' pipe in de attic.
De window a-shake, de glass near break,
De wind dat cut like razor,
De wonderin' why you never buy
De window from dat double-glazer.
De heavy coat zip to de throat,
De nose an' ears all pinky,
De weepin' sky, de clothes can't dry,
De day dem long an' inky.
De icy road, de heavy load,
De las' minute Christmas shoppin',
De cuss an' fret 'cause you feget
De ribbon an' de wrappin'.
De mud, de grime, de slush, de slime,
De place gloomy since November,
De sinkin' heart, is jus' de start o' de wintertime,
December.

Tony Bradman

I loved scary science fiction movies when I was a child, and one day found myself writing a poem that was supposed to be a trailer for a film like that — 'See the teacher reel with horror! Hear the children squeal and scream!' But then I realised I could make it funny (and disgusting), so that's what I did.

The Thing

See the teacher reel with horror!
Hear the children squeal and scream!
Watch them all retreat in terror
From The Thing that's not a dream.

Listen to the slimy sliding!
See The Thing emerge some more!
Feel the panic, watch them hiding,
Could they make it to the door?

Is The Thing an alien creature?
Is that why the classroom froze?
No… 'Get a tissue!' said the teacher.
The Thing had come… from Jason's nose!

Sandy Brownjohn

I am pleased with this poem because I was able to find a form – the nine lives of a cat – that helped me to commemorate the life of a much-loved cat without being too sentimental. It is always better to let the emotion come out of the details than to weep all over your readers!

Nine Lives
i.m. Thisbe (1976-1990)

This is my grave by the holly tree,
Remember me?

I am the cat who arrived by rail
Without a tail.

I am the cat who tried walking on water
Which would not support her.

I am the cat who got stuck on the ledge,
Too near the edge.

I am the cat who was locked in the shed
And could not be fed.

I am the cat who ran in the road
Where traffic flowed.

I am the cat who spat in the night
And lost the fight.

I am the cat who hid out in the snow
When you wanted to go.

I am the cat who with arthritic bones
Concealed her groans.

I am the cat who that Autumn day
Just faded away.

This is my grave by the holly tree.
Remember me.

James Carter

I have chosen The Dark *because it takes an everyday subject and looks at it from an unusual and fresh angle and because it is the most fun of all my poems to perform!*

—

The Dark

Why are we so afraid of the dark?
It doesn't bite and doesn't bark
Or chase old ladies round the park
Or steal your sweeties for a lark

And though it might not let you see
It lets you have some privacy
And gives you time to go to sleep
Provides a place to hide or weep

It cannot help but be around
When beastly things make beastly sounds
Or back doors slam and windows creak
And cats have fights and voices shriek

The dark is cosy, still and calm
And never does you any harm
In the loft, below the sink
It's somewhere nice and quiet to think

Deep in cupboards, pockets too
It's always lurking out of view
Why won't it come out till it's night?
Perhaps the dark's afraid of light

Charles Causley

This was the first poem I wrote specifically for children. The setting is specifically in Launceston, where I was born, by the River Kensey, a tributary of the River Tamar which divides Cornwall from Devon.

By St Thomas Water

By St Thomas Water
Where the river is thin
We looked for a jam-jar
To catch the quick fish in.
Through St Thomas Churchyard
Jessie and I ran
The day we took the jam-pot
Off the dead man.

On the scuffed tombstone
The grey flowers fell,
Cracked was the water,
Silent the shell.
The snake for an emblem
Swirled on the slab,
Across the beach of sky the sun
Crawled like a crab.

'If we walk,' said Jessie,
'Seven times round,
We shall hear a dead man
Speaking underground.'
Round the stone we danced, we sang,
Watched the sun drop,
Laid our heads and listened
At the tomb-top.

Soft as the thunder
At the storm's start
I heard a voice as clear as blood,
Strong as the heart.
But what words were spoken
I can never say,
I shut my fingers round my head,
Drove them away.

'What are those letters, Jessie,
Cut so sharp and trim
All round this holy stone
With earth up to the brim?'
Jessie traced the letters
Black as coffin-lead.
'*He is not dead but sleeping,*'
Slowly she said.

I looked at Jessie,
Jessie looked at me,
And our eyes in wonder
Grew wide as the sea.
Past the green and bending stones
We fled hand in hand,
Silent through the tongues of grass
To the river strand.

By the creaking cypress
We moved as soft as smoke
For fear all the people
Underneath awoke.
Over all the sleepers
We darted light as snow
In case they opened up their eyes,
Called us from below.

Many a day has faltered
Into many a year
Since the dead awoke and spoke
And we would not hear.
Waiting in the cold grass
Under a crinkled bough,
Quiet stone, cautious stone,
What do you tell me now?

Faustin Charles

I like the poem because it has a love and respect for animals, a sense of humour and a music which animals make all the time. The animals are alive on the page. They can be anything they want to be.

Once Upon an Animal

The bells on the toes of the birds
Are songs of the forest calling,
'Once upon an animal!'
Once upon a macaw screeching
When eagles rise and fall.
In the once upon a time world
Trees spin leaves into gold.
In the once upon a time of the deer
The animals moved without fear;
The squirrel waved a wand
And no ostrich buried its head in sand.
Once upon fur and feather
The animals loved all kinds of weather;
On rainy moonlit nights
They bathed in the bloom of watery lights.
The animals are calling,
Some tree-house homes are soaring
Into the blue webs of the spider
With wide smile of the sun
Their once upon a time days have begun.

Debjani Chatterjee

Apart from the interesting shape of the poem, I like being able to use the word 'badder' which has always struck me as a word that ought to exist; somehow 'more bad' or 'worse' just doesn't have the impact of 'badder'. I also like the nonsensical fact that the adder does yoga to make his bones 'flexible'.

Aching Bones

There's nothing badder
    than an adder
        with aching bones.
           He moans and groans,
      and hisses and bites
   and gets into fights,
over nothing.
    So something
      has to be done for the adder
        or he gets badder and madder.
      But teach him some yoga,
   he'll sway like a cobra;
tying himself in knots,
   he'll think sweet thoughts.
      There's nothing gladder
        than an adder
    who owns
flexible bones.

Gillian Clarke

In legend, a great water horse called Elidir carried seven-and-a-half men through the sea from Scotland to Wales. Seven men rode on the horse's back and one clung to his tail. One of the riders became King of North Wales. In those days the people of Wales, north-west Britain and south Scotland, which was called the Old North, all spoke one language: Welsh.

Horse of the Sea

Great water horse
whose steps are moonlight,
whose bridle is the wind,
whose mane is the wild sea,
whose whinny is the creak
of the rigging.

Black horse of ocean
whose spittle is spindrift,
whose sinews are currents,
whose skin is water,
whose bones are ships' spars,
whose heart is the drumming wave.

Horse of the sea,
seven riders on his back,
and one holding on to his tail,
brought Elidir to Gwynedd
from the lands of the Old North,
Scotland to Wales.

Du'r Moroedd.
See him tow the long salt ropes
over the sound, deeps and shallows,
and rise from the sea in a dazzle of light
on a beach in Anglesey,
to claim a Kingdom.

John Coldwell

I like the way the words reveal this cupboard to be very heavily guarded and that someone has been told not to do something but they do it anyway. I got the idea from something that happened to me when I was a boy. My grandpa told me not to look in a cupboard because he had hidden my Christmas present in there. Of course I looked but, unlike Mary, I am still here to tell the tale.

The Cupboard on the Landing

Mary had been told
Never to wipe her nose on her skirt,
Never to run in the house,
And
Never never to open the cupboard on the landing.
But one day,
After blowing her nose on a clean handkerchief,
She walked up the stairs,
Intent on opening the cupboard on the landing.

First she
Turned the key in the lock,
Then she turned the other key in the other lock,
Slid back the top bolt,
The bottom bolt
And the six bolts in between.
Then she cut through the chains,
Removed the barbed wire,
Switched off the alarm,
Threw her handkerchief over the video camera,
Undid the combination
And opened the cupboard door.

And what did Mary see
In the cupboard on the landing?
Nothing.
But something in the cupboard on the landing saw Mary.
And Mary was never seen again.

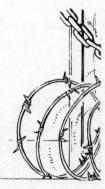

Paul Cookson

This is always a favourite because not only does it work well in its own right but it has a lot of me in the subject – wanting to be a writer of some sort, wanting to meet my heroes (Slade!), that sort of thing… Now I am a writer, I have met Slade! Noddy Holder even wrote an introduction for one of my books! And I'm working alongside poets I grew up reading and being inspired by. So there's a lot of that in there, but it's also an encouragement to anyone else who has ambitions and dreams – they can come true. I'm living proof of that. It may take a while, but if you follow your dream…

Let No-one Steal Your Dreams

Let no-one steal your dreams
Let no-one tear apart
That burning of ambition
That fires the drive inside your heart.

Let no-one steal your dreams
Let no-one tell you that you can't
Let no-one hold you back
Let no-one tell you that you won't.

Set your sights and keep them fixed
Set your sights on high
Let no-one steal your dreams
Your only limit is the sky.

Let no-one steal your dreams
Follow your heart
Follow your soul
For only when you follow them
Will you feel truly whole.

Set your sights and keep them fixed
Set your sights on high
Let no-one steal your dreams
Your only limit is the sky.

Wendy Cope

This poem was inspired by someone I'm very fond of, and that's why I'm fond of the poem. In real life this person has not actually eaten a water-lily or danced around London in his underwear. Once I had the idea for the poem, I felt free to invent some silly behaviour. I remember laughing as I wrote it.

Sensible-Bensible

Don't call me Silly Billy!
You know it's indefensible.
I wrap up when I'm chilly
And I'm sure two fives make ten.
So I'm not a silly-billy
I'm a sensible-bensible.
You're the silly-billy,
I'm a sensible-Ben.

Why do they say I'm silly?
It's quite incomprehensible.
I cackle rather shrilly
When I imitate a hen,
And I ate a water-lily
Once – I can't remember when.
But I'm not a silly-billy,
I'm a sensible-bensible.
You're the silly-billy,
I'm a sensible Ben.

I don't believe it's silly
Or rude or reprehensible
To dance down Piccadilly
In my long-johns, now and then.
My attire – warm, clean and frilly –
Is admired by other men.
You agree? Don't shally-shilly!
Must I spell it out again?
I AM NOT A SILLY-BILLY,
I'M A SENSIBLE-BENSIBLE.
Got that, Silly Billy?
Call me Sensible Ben.

Pie Corbett

I wrote this one night in an attic bedroom. I could see the rain lashing the street. The streetlight cast an orange glow. The odd car or motorbike zipped by – I couldn't see anyone driving the cars, it was almost as if the cars were alive. I remember staring at the scene, jotting the ideas down and the poem formed very quickly. I like the poem because it creates an atmosphere, brings the scene alive. I was also pleased with some of the internal rhymes that help to bind the poem together.

City Jungle

Rain splinters town.

Lizard cars cruise by;
their radiators grin.

Thin headlights stare –
shop doorways keep
their mouths shut.

At the roadside
hunched houses cough.

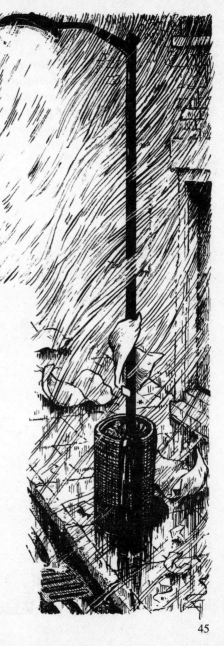

Newspapers shuffle by,
hands in their pockets.
The gutter gargles.

A motorbike snarls;
dustbins flinch.

Streetlights bare
their yellow teeth.
The motorway's
cat–black tongue
lashes across
the glistening back
of the tarmac night.

John Cotton

Oscar was an energetic, lively, cheeky and often naughty Jack Russell, with a distinct personality of his own, and who frequently disrupted my life! The poem came, as poems often do, from observing him and thinking about his general cheekiness! I chose the poem as one I like because it reminds me of him and helps me to remember him.

Oscar the Dog

I'm Oscar the Dog
I'm my own dog not theirs –
In spite of whatever they think.
So I'll fight and I'll run
And have lots of fun,
And find dirty puddles to drink.

I'm Oscar the Dog
And my breed's Dartmoor Terrier,
And let me tell you for free,
That I'll bark and I'll pull,
And I'm never the merrier
Than sniffing and being just me.

I'm Oscar the Dog
And when I am called
I keep them all waiting a while.
Though I go in the end
I like to pretend
I'll run off, 'cause that is my style.

I'm Oscar the Dog
And I'm all for Dogs' Lib,
Though my mistress tells people I'm good.
So I growl at her friends
And water her plants
To make sure it's quite understood

That I'm Oscar the Dog
And when I'm called bad
I smile and I wag my small tail,
And as for a smack,
It's like a pat on the back,
I tell you it really can't fail!

I'm Oscar the Dog
And I'm everyone's friend
When there's something to offer or give,
A biscuit or tit bit,
I really don't mind,
After all a dog's got to live.

Sue Cowling

It's satisfying to see how much you can say in a few words. A sound, a feeling and an image are encapsulated in this tiny poem.

Leaves

My wellingtons swish
through the leaves.
I am four years old again, at play
in the crumpled wrapping paper
of the year.

Kevin Crossley-Holland

It's one of my favourites because it helps me to remember one of the most amazing places on earth – the church at Acoma (which means Sky City) in New Mexico. The church and the adobe houses surrounding it are perched on a rock seven hundred feet above the burning desert floor. In the early seventeenth century, one of the first Catholic missionary priests of St Estevan of Acoma persuaded the Navajo to sell four boys and four girls into slavery to raise money for the church bell.

The Desert Singer

When the sandstone Navajo
tugs the huge church bell
the desert brightness trembles
at what its deep voices tell:

'I was bought with children.
I cost them their laughing years.
My price was their freedom,
I glisten with their tears.

I am cast in Spanish bronze
and weigh upward of two tons.
Heavy the heart which beats to
the sale of Navajo daughters and sons.

I toll the dirge of slavery
and I pulse with young, bright blood.
I'm tempered by fierce desert frost
that stabs flowers in the bud.'

Again the sandstone Navajo
swings the grand church bell:
'I am guilt but I am hope:
all manner of thing shall be well.

Choose right and do right,
you who do daily wrong.
I am the desert singer
and you are my suffering song.'

People pray on the mesa
and they pause on the burning plain
as the church bell wags its tongue
and, shuddering, insists again:

'My poor, longing people!
Each life is a quilt
in which right redeems wrong.
Shining deeds atone for guilt.

Here, on creaking knee-bones,
your forebears sobbed for their kin,
and knocked a hole in the church wall
to let the spirits back in

– the spirits of all their children
released, and ghosting home,
sweet voices rising and quavering,
and one now with my own.'

John Cunliffe

I've chosen this poem because it is great fun to read to children on school visits and at festivals: the blood-curdling shriek at the end gives everyone a fright, then they all fall about laughing helplessly. If the audience is shy and nervous about meeting an author it breaks the ice in a trice.

If You Come to Our House

If you come to our house
In the middle of the night,
You're sure to get
A terrible fright.
It's choc-a-bloc full
Of ghosts, you see,
But whatever they do,
They can't scare me!

There are two little baby ghosts
Playing on the stairs,
And a headless horseman
Saying his prayers;
And a spook in the toilet
Having a pee,
But whatever they do,
They can't scare me!

There's a ghoul in the garden,
Playing with the cat,
And another on the patio,
Wearing granny's hat;
Apparitions in the kitchen,
Having their tea,
But whatever they do,
They can't scare me!

There's a boggart in the chimney
Blowing up the fire,
And a cellar-full of spirits,
All singing in a choir.
There are zombies in the parlour,
Watching TV,
But whatever they do,
They can't scare me!

If you come to our house
In the middle of the night,
You're sure to get
An awful fright.
It's choc-a-bloc full
Of ghosts, you see,
But… whatever… they… do…,
But whatever they…
But what ever…!
But what…!
But……………………..
Aaaaaaaaaaaaaarrrrrrrrgggggghhhhhhh!

Jan Dean

I like this poem for two reasons. I enjoy the rhythm of it and often use it to start performances – great fun. Also it's a 'true' poem. I don't mean that this actually happened exactly as it's written here, but the feelings in it are absolutely true. When I wrote it I used the story of my husband cheating in the potato and spoon race (by sellotaping the spud to the spoon!) and I mixed it with the terrible feeling I had when I got the swimming team disqualified. Writers mix up facts and feelings all the time to make 'new' stories and poems – and that's what I did here.

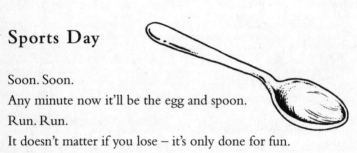

Sports Day

Soon. Soon.

Any minute now it'll be the egg and spoon.

Run. Run.

It doesn't matter if you lose – it's only done for fun.

Lies. Lies.

The winner is the one who gets the prize,

The loser gets a slow-hand-clap and then sits down and cries.

Cheat. Cheat.

I hear the awful chanting and I trip on my own feet.

Dumb. Dumb.

I really didn't know you couldn't grip it with your thumb…

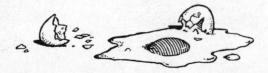

Peter Dixon

It's good to laugh and smile a lot, and funny poems are enjoyable to read and write. But it's important to write about sad or worrying things as well.

Biento

For three years Biento cried.
Sometimes he played,
but mostly he cried.
Biento was always, always
hungry
and on his third birthday
Biento died.
When he played he liked to laugh.
When he was dying
he did not cry,
he just stared at the floor.
Biento's dad put Biento in a black plastic bag,
the sort mum puts our rubbish in.
His name was Biento.
Biento means Sunshine.

Berlie Doherty

The first time I saw a badger, I was still living in a city, Sheffield. A friend took me to a badger sett in Derbyshire, promising me I would see one. We seemed to wait for hours! But at last the badger came, and it was as if a spell had been cast on me. Now I live in Derbyshire and often see badgers – and it's always a thrill.

Badger

Through the trees I saw a badger
Early evening, nearly dusk
All the midges dancing round me
Foxglove scent, and ferny musk.

Through the trees I saw a badger
In the twilight, stars just out
Bats like rags were drifting, swooping
Sheep on hillside, farmer's shout.

Through the trees I saw a badger
Through the air as grey as smoke
Light as dancers she came listening
Light as ghosts she sniffed the dark.

Through the trees I saw a badger
Barred head lifted, wary, keen,
Then she faded through the bracken
Like a whisper, like a dream.

Gina Douthwaite

Messing about with the English language is as much fun for me as it is for a rhino to wallow in mud. I guess we both tend to get stuck at times but when RHINO sets like concrete and my words flow, then, together, we've shaped up to expectations. That feels good.

Rhino

becomes When more than one rhinoceros
rhinoceroses, and each of these
has horns of hair that stick up from their
noses, and armoured skin that wallows in
the mud when they reposes, and on each
foot each rhino has three hooves
instead of toeses – the
of these creatures show features
the problem language poses
when more be-
than one comes
rhino- rhinoc-
ceros eroses.

Carol Ann Duffy

This is one of my favourite poems because it grew from a conversation with my six-year-old daughter and makes me think of being a mother and having been a child.

The Cord
for Ella

They cut the cord I was born with
and buried it under a tree
in the heart of the Great Forest
when I was only wee,
the length of my mother's elbow
to the tip of her thumb.

I learned to speak and asked them,
though I was very young,
what the cord had looked like –
had a princess spun it
from a golden spinning-wheel?
Or was the cord silver? Was it real?

Real enough and buried
in the roots of an ancient oak,
the tangled knot of a riddle
or the weird ribbon of a gift
in a poke. When I grew, I asked again
if the cord was made of rope,

then stared from the house I lived in
across the fields to the woods
where rooks spread their pages of wings
like black unreadable books
and the wind in the grass
scribbled sentences wherever I looked.

So I went on foot to the forest
and pressed my ear to the ground,
but not a sound or a movement,
not a breath or a word
gave me hint where I should go
to hunt for my cord. I went deeper

into the forest, following a bird
which disappeared, a waving hand; shadows
blurred into one huge darkness,
but the stars were my mother's eyes
and the screech of an owl in the tree above
was the sound of a baby's cry.

Michael Dugan

'It's raining cats and dogs' was a favourite saying of my mother's when I was a boy. One day I decided to write a poem around her and her saying which is why it is one of my favourites.

Sound Advice

'Come inside at once,' Mum said.
'Get out of all that rain.'
'We're having fun,' was our reply,
'don't be such a pain.'

'It's raining cats and dogs,' Mum cried.
I told her, 'Don't be silly.'
Just then a sopping Labrador
squashed flat my brother Willie.

Helen Dunmore

I have chosen Smiles Like Roses *because it is about the joy of living. It brings back those first hot days of the year, when everyone opens their windows, puts on summer clothes and starts smiling.*

Smiles Like Roses

All down my street
smiles opened like roses
sun licked me and tickled me
sun said, Didn't you believe me
when I said I'd be back?

I blinked my eyes, I said,
Sun, you are too strong for me
where'd you get those muscles?
Sun said, Come and dance.

All over the park
smiles opened like roses
babies kicked off their shoes
and sun kissed their toes.

All those new babies
all that new sun
everybody dancing
walking but dancing.

All over the world
sun kicked off his shoes
and came home dancing
licking and tickling

kissing crossing-ladies and fat babies
saying to everyone
*Hey you are the most beautiful
dancing people I've ever seen
with those smiles like roses!*

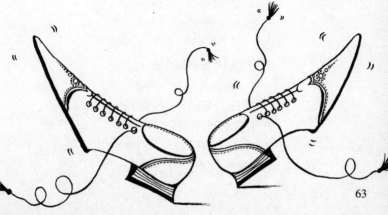

Richard Edwards

I have always liked to write about 'things' as well as people, and have tried to imagine what 'things' might do and feel when no-one is watching. In this poem two old things, thrown out on a rubbish dump, fall in love.

The Glove and the Guitar

A toy guitar
And an old green glove
Meeting on the rubbish dump
Fell in love.

'How smooth, how plump,
How curved you are,'
Said the old green glove
To the toy guitar.

Said the toy guitar,
'My dusty heart sings
When I think of your fingers
Tickling my strings.'

Dusk and darkness
And, oh, what a fright
The neighbourhood tom-cats
Got that night,

When they heard from the dump
Strange sounds coming,
Sounds of plucking,
Sounds of strumming,

Sounds of a wild
Flamenco tune,
As the glove and the toy guitar
Played beneath the moon.

Max Fatchen

I always thought as a child the breeze made a sad and weary little sound as it blew through our wirescreen on a warm Australian day. So this poem revives the memories of my Australian country childhood.

Windy Work

Weary breeze through my window screen,
Where are you going and where have you been?

I cooled the sweat on a farmer's brow
And fanned the dreams of a dozing cow.
I played a tune on the telephone wires
And rocked the trees for the magpie choirs.
I shook the stalks of the long-eared wheat
And they danced the paddock off its feet.

I passed a train with its diesel smell.
I caught the clang of the crossing bell.
I tumbled the bushes and made them roll
And fluttered the flag on a schoolyard pole.
I carried the children's lunch-hour shout,
No wonder a breeze is a bit puffed out.

I rushed and rippled a placid dam.
I stroked the grass and here I am.
I climbed the range and each rock-ridged hill
So may I rest on your windowsill?

Eric Finney

This poem brings back memories of a sponsored walk on which the girl of nine or ten with whom I was walking displayed an astonishing knowledge of wild flowers. Asked how she'd become so knowledgeable, she said, 'Oh, my granny taught me flowers.' It was years later that this stored experience became the poem.

Learning the Flowers

Along the lanes, down sunny hours,
That summer Granny taught me flowers:
Dog rose, foxglove, lady's smock,
Ox-eye daisy, townhall clock,
Billy's button, adder's meat,
Old man's beard and meadowsweet.
Sometimes I went to pick, but she
Smiled and said gently, 'Let them be,'
Sticky Willy, bugle, pansy,
Yellow rattle, harebell, tansy,
Silverweed and tormentil:
She taught me and I know them still.

John Foster

I've chosen this poem because it deals with an issue that concerns everybody and about which we must all make up our own minds. I think it's important that there should be poems that deal with serious subjects such as this.

—

'It Isn't Right to Fight'

You said, 'It isn't right to fight.'
But when we watched the news tonight,
You shook your fist and said
You wished the tyrant and his cronies dead.
When I asked why,
If it's not right to fight,
You gave a sigh.
You shook your head
And sadly said,
'Sometimes a cause is just
And, if there is no other way,
Perhaps, you must.'

Pam Gidney

Don't you wish this could happen to a bully you know? But we don't all have a witch for an aunt! Even though I wrote it, I still giggle every time I get to the last verse! I'm sure Harriet would never have kissed Henry when he was a boy, and certainly not when he was a frog! So I suppose he is sitting there still on his lily pad, wishing he had been nicer to Harriet.

Horrible Henry

Henry was hateful, spiteful, bad,
Teased the girls and made them mad.

Horrible Henry hated Harriet
(Popular, pretty, happy-as-Larry-et).

Henry tied poor Harriet's hair
(Two long plaits) to the back of her chair.

Stole her dinner-money, hid her shoes,
Locked her up inside the loos.

Henry boasted: 'My Dad's rich.'
Harriet said, 'My Aunt's a witch.'

Henry said, 'From what I've learnt
Ain't no witches. All got burnt.'

'Not my Auntie Dorothea,'
Harriet said, and went to see her.

Dorothea waved her wand.
Henry landed in a pond.

Green and slimy, hopping mad,
He sits upon a lily pad

Croaking loudly in Frogese,
'Kiss me, Harriet! Kiss me, please!'

Mick Gowar

In this poem I've tried to portray the complex relationship that I think a lot of boys have with football. The terrible truth is that although you may be keen, and you practise and train, you may still not be any good. And the vast majority of fans are not any good at playing football. Unfortunately, professionalism – in the worst senses of the word – has infected so many sports (and other areas of life) that people who want to have a go at a sport, or paint a picture or make music – people who simply want to join in and enjoy themselves despite their lack of talent – are too often ridiculed instead of being praised and encouraged.

Boots

It's chilly on the touch line, but
with all my kit on
underneath my clothes
I'm not too cold. Besides,
I've got a job to do:

> I'm Third Reserve.
> I run the line.

I've been the Third Reserve all season,
every Saturday.
I've never missed a match:
at Home, Away
it's all the same to me

> 'cos I'm the Third Reserve.
> The bloke who runs the line.

That's my reward
for turning up
to every practice session, every
circuit training. Everything.
No one else does that
       to be the Third Reserve,
       to run the line.

No chance of substitutions.
Broken ankles on the pitch
mean someone else's chance, not mine.
One down
            and still two more to go:
       when you're the Third Reserve
       you run the line.

When I was first made Third Reserve
my dad and me went out
and bought new boots. I keep them in the box.
I grease them every week and put them back.
       When you're the Third Reserve
          you know the score:
       you run the line in worn-out daps.

David Harmer

One reason this is a favourite is that after writing a series of poems with a complicated rhyming structure, to write in free verse came as an enjoyable and refreshing change. The other main reason is that the poem puts children in charge of things. I have read the poem to a lot of different groups of children and not one of them has disagreed with my new laws! In this poem, the children have all the power and the grown-ups have to do as they are told. It's about time.

The Prime Minister is Ten Today

10 DOWNING ST

This morning I abolished
homework, detention and dinner ladies.
I outlawed lumpy custard, school mashed spuds
and handwriting lessons.
From now on playtimes must last two hours
unless it rains, in which case we all go home
except the teachers who must do extra PE
outside in the downpour.

Whispering behind your hand in class
must happen each morning between ten and twelve,
and each child need only do
ten minutes' work in one school hour.

I've passed a No Grumpy Teacher law
so one bad word or dismal frown
from Mr Spite or Miss Hatchetface
will get them each a month's stretch
sharpening pencils and marking books
inside the gaol of their choice.

All headteachers are forbidden
from wearing soft-soled shoes,
instead they must wear wooden clogs
so you can hear them coming.
They are also banned from shouting
or spoiling our assembly by pointing
at the ones who never listen.

Finally, the schools must shut
for at least half the year
and if the weather's really sunny
the teachers have to take us all
to the seaside for the day.

If you've got some good ideas
for other laws about the grown-ups
drop me a line in Downing Street,
I'll always be glad to listen.
Come on, help me change a thing or two
before we all grow up
and get boring.

Michael Harrison

I've kept a diary every day for about twenty years and it's never as interesting as I want it to be. This poem reminds me of the huge gap that is always there between what I want to say and what actually gets down on paper.

Diary

Got up, went to school,
did homework, went to bed.

All that is net: life's
quick fish escaped.

Anne Harvey

Miss Simpkins — not her real name — was my Geography teacher at school, and not a very stimulating one. She was a sad lady — I was cheeky to her — and then, years later, felt guilty. The poem is true.

Miss Simpkins

It couldn't have been you
queuing for your pension
in the post-office last Monday
though the limp dress and scraped back bun
reminded me of you.

I watched you down the street
move like a startled hen
and I recalled dull Geography lessons
when Miss Simpkins' dreary voice
droned on expressionless.

She had no gift for teaching;
countries were pastel shapes,
wiggly blue lines for rivers,
words like oasis, strata, hemisphere,
fell on deaf ears.

Boredom hung thick in yawns
and, as I doodled,
a caricature with skinny legs,
large feet, lank hair,
formed on my rough-book page.

I never thought she'd look,
pale eyes watery, pink-spotted cheeks,
thin wavery voice:
'And who's this meant to be?'
'You, Miss Simpkins, can't you see!'

A few weeks later
when it was Founders' Day
The school was hung with photographs
offering us a taste
of life in days gone by,

And in one dated thirty years ago
There was Miss Simpkins,
a new teacher at the school,
same hair, same chicken look, same dress,
and looking just as old.

At Christmas time I took Miss Simpkins flowers
when no-one saw,
tried not to catch her eye,
and very soon she left
to nurse an ageing father, someone said.

It couldn't have been you
I saw last Monday in the post-office
for in the Old Girls' magazine
under Obituaries
I noticed you were dead.

John Hegley

The person who seems to be the goodie (in this case uncle) may not be as good as you might think from their picture. Sometimes adults don't understand the deepness of a child's feeling and seeing. The child can know exactly how good their work is: very good, quite good, very quite good and not very good at all.

Uncle and Auntie

My auntie gives me a colouring book and crayons.
I choose the picture of the puppies in a wicker basket.
I begin to colour.
After a while Auntie leans over to see what I have done
and says, 'You've gone over the lines,
that's what you've done!
What do you think they're there for, eh?
Some kind of statement is it?
Going to be a rebel are we?
Your auntie's given you a nice present
and you've gone and spoilt it.'
I begin to cry.
My uncle gives me a hanky and some blank paper.
'Do some doggies of your own,' he says.
I begin to colour.
When I have done
he looks over
and says they are all very good.
He is lying;
only some of them are.

Stewart Henderson

We often go through the day feeling so much inside but are not always able to put it into words. It's a poem about wanting to rise above those 'grumbly' feelings we sometimes have. We can take comfort in our imagination and realise that life is big and good, and we don't have to be 'hemmed in' by what can turn out to be just passing feelings.

Sometimes

Sometimes I don't like myself
but then sometimes I do,
and sometimes it's so hard to know
if what I feel is true.

Like when I have a tantrum,
is that all people see?
I'm only like that sometimes,
that fury's not all me.

Sometimes I go racing through
the playground in my head,
which is awkward if I should
be doing geography instead.

Those 'sometimes' I go missing
while my body is still here,
they're much the best of sometimes –
that's when I disappear.

For then I go all over
from Ecuador to Mars,
to nesting with the eagle
and swapping round the stars.

That magic sometimes when I feel
beyond the moon and free,
the sometimes I forget myself
and let myself be me.

Diana Hendry

I came upon Cullen Skink in a Scottish cookery book. It's really a dish of smoked haddock, but I imagined it was the name of a strange creature. I like the poem's mystery. I like the idea of someone 'skinking' and the poem says quite a lot about how I often feel inside.

The Cullen Skink

If the temperature's right
you might see him out
in a very fine suit
of the best bravado,
but skinking with caution
for his eyesight's poor
and he's all out of proportion.

Unshelled, in the buff,
his raw-pink skin
is prone to shrinkage
which is why he lets no-one in
and lives far north, alone
in a nest of coddled mementoes
kept on simmer. Some say
it's the Cullen Skink's nature
to shiver and to be perpetually
on the brink of some great thought
he never delivers.

He likes to drink.
He likes to look at the moon.
At night you can hear the clink
as he walks the jetty
trailing a kind of umbilical cord,
the dried-up remnants
of wings, fur, paws.

Russell Hoban

This one gives me goose pimples. I'm haunted by the bone whistle and the drum calling up the ghosts of long-dead horses. I hear hoofbeats, the twang of the ghost rider's bow and the hiss of the arrow.

The Ghost Horse of Chingis Khan

Chingis, Chingis, Chingis Khan,
galloping, galloping, galloping –
Chingis, Chingis, Chingis Khan,
where is the hill he lies upon?
Nobody knows.

Under what lost and lonely star,
galloping, galloping, galloping far,
galloping where the ghost herds are?
Nobody knows.

Thousands of horses now are one,
galloping, galloping, galloping.
Call with a whistle made of bone,
call up the bay, the grey, the roan,
ee-lu-lu-ee-ya-ee, now come,
come to my whistle, come to my drum,
come with the ghost of Chingis Khan,
strong on the herds he rode upon –
thousand of horses now are one,
ee-lu-lu-ee-ya-ee!

Under the moon, under the sun,
thousands of horses now are one;
thousands of days are one long night –
look with the dark, look with the bright,
look for the ghost of Chingis Khan,
strong on the horse he rode upon –
ee-lu-lu-ee-ya-ee!

Red is the ghost horse, red like flame,
bright in the darkness – speak its name,
keen as the bend of the Tartar bow,
galloping, galloping. Who can know
the name of the horse he rides upon?
Chingis, Chingis, Chingis Khan!

Libby Houston

I've always loved narrative poems, ballads, their legends and fairy stories. Especially as I've been haunted by those entailing severe, often (apparently) unjust, punishments – I've written some like that myself. This is for once a light-hearted tribute to the tradition. It has an admirable moral and may be my shortest story.

The Old Woman and the Sandwiches

I met a wizened wood-woman
    Who begged a crumb of me.
Four sandwiches of ham I had:
    I gave her three.

'Bless you, thank you, kindly Miss –
    Shall be rewarded well –
Three everlasting gifts, whose value
    None can tell.'

'Three wishes?' out I cried in glee.
    'No, gifts you may not choose:
A flea and gnat to bite your back
    And gravel in your shoes.'

Robert Hull

I like this because it reminds me of someone I know talking, and because I think it's a good reason for being off school.

Dear Mrs James

Dear Mrs James,
I've desided to keep mum at home today.
School and everything's getting her down,
she's got parent burnout, it's all got too much,
what with as well as takeing me and Ed
and Danny and Jane next door in every day
and bringing us home, Tuesdays
she collects me after my guitarrh lesson
and waits while Danny has maths coatching
round Mr Fellows' house then Wedensdays
is my football practise plus a lift
to evening rehersals for Ed for Cats
in the village hall. Thursdays after school
is extra tests for Sats for me, and Fridays
before school it's speling club which dad says
I have to go to I don't see why. Saturday morning
their's football a match and Saturday afternoon
we go family shopping. So I rung up the docter
and asked can she give mum some rest pills
or something but she says to take her out for lunch
on the bus with money from dad and go shopping
for clothes or something and get some flowers
and keep her away from the car which is what
we're doing. So I'm not coming into school today
or tomorrow probably because this is inportant
I know youll agree and be simperthetic,
take care, see you Monday, *love, Melissa*.

Jenny Joseph

I am pleased with The Hunter Evades the Guardians *because I enjoyed getting the rhymes and repetitions of sound right without stopping the sentence. I am also quite pleased with the horrid old man I've made, sitting in his greenhouse, and his wild lawless enemy who is his equal.*

The Hunter Evades the Guardians

Pit pat tabby cat
Tip top pitapat
Tiptoed through the grass
Up and over
The wall
That straight and tall
And spiked with glass
Held the garden.

Hidden in a green-house
Closed in by darkness
Man and long-haired pussy-cat
Ill-intentioned, waiting:
A snarl
Oh well-kept puss, a gnarl
On an old hand that
Clutched a truncheon.

'Pst here he comes now
Just watch and see how
He takes my birds, my mice.'
'Digging up my seedlings!
Vandal –
What a scandal!
Deep-dyed vice
Must be dealt with.'

Proud lithe animal
Silkily along the wall
Untouched by glinting glass
Noticed his enemies.
He leapt
A shadow crept
Behind tall grass
Into the garden.

Mike Jubb

I am in love... with the English language. I particularly love playing with words through anagrams, palindromes, homophones, rhyming slang, spoonerisms, word-morphing and, especially, puns. A pun has been described as a short quip, followed by a long groan. Do the puns in my poem make you want to groan?

School is Closed Today Because...

School is closed today because…

The Geography teacher got lost
The History teacher had a date
The R.E. teacher couldn't believe it
The Cookery teacher got stuffed
The Science teacher was a physical wreck
The Art teacher got the wrong impression
The P.E. teacher was unfit for the job
The Maths teacher had divided loyalties
The Woodwork teacher took a plane
The Music teacher went flat
The English teacher was written off
The French teacher went inseine

And then we all lost our Head.

Jackie Kay

This poem is about a real imaginary friend I had when I was young. My family believed he actually existed for two years so that even now the word for lie in my family is 'Brendon Gallacher'. It's my favourite because it reminds me of my imaginary friend and how poetry is about making things up.

Brendon Gallacher

He was seven and I was six, my Brendon Gallacher.
He was Irish and I was Scottish, my Brendon Gallacher.
His father was in prison; he was a cat burglar.
My father was a communist party full-time worker.
He had six brothers and I had one, my Brendon Gallacher.

He would hold my hand and take me by the river
where we'd talk all about his family being poor.
He'd get his mum out of Glasgow when he got older.
A wee holiday some place nice. Some place far.
I'd tell my mum about my Brendon Gallacher

How his mum drank and his daddy was a cat burglar.
And she'd say, 'Why not have him round to dinner?'
No, no, I'd say he's got big holes in his trousers.
I like meeting him by the burn in the open air.
Then one day after we'd been friends for two years,

One day when it was pouring and I was indoors,
my mum says to me, 'I was talking to Mrs Moir
who lives next door to your Brendon Gallacher
Didn't you say his address was 24 Novar?
She says there are no Gallachers at 24 Novar

There never have been any Gallachers next door.'
And he died then, my Brendon Gallacher,
flat out on my bedroom floor, his spiky hair,
his impish grin, his funning flapping ear.
Oh Brendon. Oh my Brendon Gallacher.

Daphne Kitching

I wrote this poem soon after moving house. I had moved from living in a familiar place where I had been very happy, to an unknown area, and I didn't know if I would like it. On my first walk, I found a bench which was so high that, when I sat on it, my feet couldn't touch the ground – they just had to swing! It reminded me of being a child, with legs that always swing! It is an optimistic poem. It makes me realise that no matter how much we enjoy where we are now, there are always new adventures and exciting times waiting for us over the next wall!

Growing Up

I don't want to grow up,
With legs that won't swing
When I sit on a bench,
Like my Dad.
And who wants to walk
When it's more fun to skip?
As people grow old
They grow sad.

I want to stand on my head
When the feeling comes on,
And blow bubbles with gum
Till it pops.
I want to cry when things hurt me,
To be cuddled and held,
And to know that
The loving won't stop.

I don't want to grow up,
But everyone does,
As the years pass
I'm getting quite tall.
And though my legs soon won't swing
On the bench,
The *good* thing is…
I now can see over the wall!

John Kitching

I quite like the neatness of this little sequence of haikus, written in an attempt to catch some key pictures of the seasons in just sixty-eight syllables.

Haiku Year

Summer. Lazy days.
Only the bees seem busy.
Purple plums ripen.

Autumn. Leaves wither,
Fade and spiral slowly down.
Bold blackberries bulge.

Winter. Under snow
And grey ice, the world seems dead.
The chill air is still.

Spring. Early birds call.
Father sharpens rusty shears.
Life begins again.

Tony Langham

This poem is about communication and its importance in our lives. Poets have to be good communicators. Animals are wonderful communicators. Wouldn't it be fantastic if we could learn their languages – think of the poems which could be written! Move over Dr. Dolittle!

Linguist

Can you speak cockroach? – I can
And I'm fluent in kangaroo too,
I've learned how to talk to animals
By listening to them down at the zoo.

I started with birds 'cos they're chatty,
They've always got something to say
And if you listen quite carefully
You can learn what you need in a day.

Quite soon I was talking to finches,
Parrots, flamingo and fowl,
But I knew I'd made a real breakthrough
When I toowhit-toowhooed with an owl.

After that I conversed with some mammals.
I began with mouse, gerbil and rat,
Quickly picked up mole, vole and squirrel
Then learned how to chat in pure cat.

I learned lion, tiger and cheetah,
Zebra, antelope, baboon, chimp and of course,
Together with giraffe, rhino and hippo,
I could soon discourse with a horse.

Doggy dialects by the dozen, I then mastered.
I learnt Labrador, sheep-dog and Great Dane.
I practised pronunciation with beagles,
But talking poodle was rather a strain.

To creatures cold-blooded I moved on then,
Speaking with reptiles of all kinds
And discovered through prolonged conversations
That lizards and snakes have fine minds.

I soon became fluent with amphibians,
Learned to croak in frog and in toad,
Learned to speak newt with an accent that's cute,
Communicated with salamanders in code!

Fish too hold great conversations,
But here, let me give you some tips;
Keep your mouth closed when underwater
And learn how to read fishy lips.

At sea I talked with cetaceans,
With porpoises, dolphins, great whales –
How lovely it was to float, listening
To their fabulous deep ocean tales.

Their singing too was delightful,
By day and by night they all croon,
In calm or tempestuous weather,
Beneath the sun and the moon.

Now I'm learning to speak with the insects
And other creatures which creep, crawl and slide –
I've mastered cockroach, beetle and spider
And speak slug with considerable pride.

Now you might ask why I have bothered,
You might ask and in reply I would say,
Learning any language is time never wasted;
It might just come in useful one day.

And the more we talk to each other,
Regardless of species or race,
Will make our lives that little bit richer
And the world a happier place!

Dennis Lee

I don't have a single favourite among my poems. But I like the way The Question *sings, and I like the way there's something hidden inside it, something about how friendships happen.*

The Question

If I could teach you how to fly
Or bake an elderberry pie
Or turn the sidewalk into stars
Or play new songs on an old guitar
Or if I knew the way to heaven
The names of night, the taste of seven
And owned them all, to keep or lend –
Would you come and be my friend?

You cannot teach me how to fly.
I love the berries but not the pie.
The sidewalks are for walking on,
And an old guitar has just one song.
The names of night cannot be known,
The way to heaven cannot be shown.
You cannot keep, you cannot lend –
But still I want you for my friend.

Patricia Leighton

I had a lot of fun writing this. I like imagining the whole crazy scene as if it is an animated cartoon. I think the rhythm and rhyme help set the mood, too.

The Rock Pool Rock

There's a riot in the rock pool,
The crabs are linking claws,
Throwing up their legs and dancing
Can-cans with the prawns.
An ancient purple lobster
Is deejaying the affair
But no-one takes much notice
– it's as if he isn't there!

The tentacled anemones
Are swinging to the beat
Of all the little winkles
Stamping all their little feet;
The cockle shells and limpets
Pull apart and then collide,
And a row of flirty seaworms
Does the slinky 'Rock Pool Glide'.

The mussel boys are posing
In tuxedos, shiny blue,
A snazzy razor shell pops up
And yells, 'Hi, lads, what's new?'
Yeh, it's rocking in the rock pool,
It's a swinging seashore jam.
Hey, don't take off your shoes
And put your toes in –

                    cool it, man!

J. Patrick Lewis

In Stories, *I wanted to evoke a phantom memory about a boy and his dog — a golden retriever, in my mind — that would speak of the abiding bond between the two. In fact, the poem is about the dog I never had.*

Stories

Circling by the fire,
My dog, my rough champion,
Coaxes winter out of her fur.
She hears old stories
Leaping in the flames:
The hissing names of cats,
Neighbours' dogs snapping
Like these gone logs,
The cracking of ice…
Once, romping through the park,
We dared the creaking pond.
It took the dare and half
Of me into the dark below.
She never let go.

We watch orange tongues
Wagging in the fire
Hush to blue whispers.
Her tail buffs my shoe.
She has one winter left.

Maybe two.

John Lyons

This poem celebrates a happy, playful, childhood energy as expressed symbolically in the words which describe the flight of this simple, easy-to-make paper kite.

Chickichong

My cheeky chickichong
giddying-up with tipsy butterflies
zigzagging over zinnias.

In the shut-in gallery
I am as free as my brown paper kite
playing with the wind,
tail a crazy thing
without zwill,
without sting,
zingaytaying
in a whistled
breeze.

Lindsay MacRae

I really love puns and the peculiarities of the English language which is why I like this poem. When I can't sleep I like to make up as many 'knock knock' jokes as I can or else imagine what an umbrella might be if it wasn't something to keep you dry.

The Babysitter

It was clear
From the moment
They walked out the door
That Tracey
Had never done
This job before.

Until they came home
She patiently sat
On me
      my little brother
           and the cat.

Roger McGough

Many of my poems are light and funny, and often the starting point is an unusual use of language. But here I am in a more serious mood (you might even say religious) where I am contrasting good and evil, and warning of the dangers of cynicism and envy.

The Man Who Steals Dreams

Santa Claus has a brother
A fact few people know
He does not have a friendly face
Or a beard as white as snow

He does not climb down chimneys
Or ride in an open sleigh
He is not kind and giving
But cruelly takes away

He is not fond of children
Or grown-ups who are kind
And emptiness the only gift
That he will leave behind

He is wraith, he is silent
He is greyness of steam
And if you're sleeping well tonight
Then hang on to your dream

He is sour, he is stooping
His cynic's cloak is black
And if he takes your dream away
You never get it back

Dreams with happy endings
With ambition and joy
Are the ones that he seeks
To capture and destroy

So, if you don't believe in Santa
Or in anything at all
The chances are his brother
Has already paid a call

Ian McMillan

I love this poem. I love the rhyme, the rhythm, the daftness, the images. It's one of those poems that I spent ages writing, ages getting right. I love that 'boiled eggs with deserters' joke! I'm going to have this poem on my gravestone when I die!

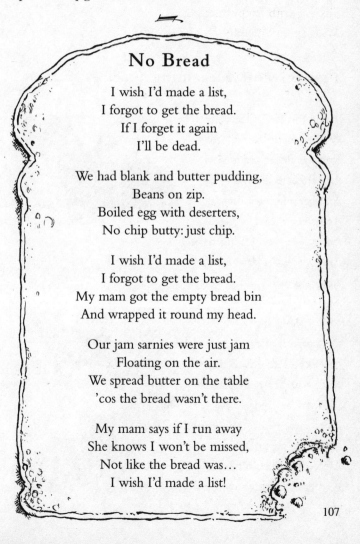

No Bread

I wish I'd made a list,
I forgot to get the bread.
If I forget it again
I'll be dead.

We had blank and butter pudding,
Beans on zip.
Boiled egg with deserters,
No chip butty: just chip.

I wish I'd made a list,
I forgot to get the bread.
My mam got the empty bread bin
And wrapped it round my head.

Our jam sarnies were just jam
Floating on the air.
We spread butter on the table
'cos the bread wasn't there.

My mam says if I run away
She knows I won't be missed,
Not like the bread was…
I wish I'd made a list!

Colin McNaughton

In performance I say to my audience that this will probably be the most horrible poem they'll ever hear. That's mainly because I sing it and my singing voice is truly the stuff of nightmares, but also because this really is a thoroughly unpleasant piece.

Transylvania Dreaming (cert PG)

In the middle of the night
When you're safe in bed
And the doors are locked
And the cats are fed
And it's much too bright
And sleep won't come
And there's something wrong
And you want your mom
And you hear a noise
And you see a shape
And it looks like a bat
Or a man in a cape
And you dare not breathe
And your heart skips a beat
And you're cold as ice
From your head to your feet
And you say a prayer
And you swear to be good
And you'd run for your life

If you only could
And your eyes are wide
And stuck on stalks
As the thing in black
Toward you walks
And the room goes dark
And you faint clean away
And you don't wake up
Till the very next day...

And you open your eyes
And the sun is out
And you jump out of bed
And you sing and shout,
'It was only a dream!'
And you dance around the room
And your heart is as light
As a helium balloon
And your mom rushes in
And says, 'Hold on a sec...

What are those two little
Holes in your neck?'

Wes Magee

This poem records an actual event, and is a memorial for a pupil in a school where I taught. I like the way the single sound rhyme (there/care/there/hair/dare, etc.) and the repeated line at the end of each verse help to create a feeling of sadness.

Tracey's Tree

Last year it was not there,
the sapling with purple leaves
planted in the school grounds with care.
It's Tracey's tree, my friend who died,
and last year it was not there.

Tracey the girl with long black hair,
who, out playing one day, ran
across a main road for a dare.
The lorry struck her. Now a tree grows
and last year it was not there.

Through the classroom window I stare
and watch the sapling sway.
Soon its branches will stand bare.
It wears a forlorn and lonely look
and last year it was not there.

October's chill is in the air
and cold rain distorts my view.
I feel a sadness that's hard to bear.
The tree blurs, as if I've been crying,
and last year it was not there.

Margaret Mahy

Cat in the Dark is a favourite of mine, because as a cat owner, I think it catches a certain mood. As evening falls, cats often change from being curled-up, sleepy-afternoon animals into mysterious spirits haunting the shadows, and doing sneaky dances on the edge of night. I think the poem catches the mood of this transformation.

Cat in the Dark

Mother, Mother, what was that?
Hush, my darling! Only the cat.
(Fighty-bitey, ever-so-mighty)
Out in the moony dark.

Mother, Mother, what was that?
Hush, my darling! Only the cat.
(Prowly-yowly, sleepy-creepy,
Fighty-bitey, ever-so-mighty)
Out in the moony dark.

Mother, Mother, what was that?
Hush, my darling! Only the cat.
(Sneaky-peeky, cosy-dozy,
Prowly-yowly, sleepy-creepy,
Fighty-bitey, ever-so-mighty)
Out in the moony dark.

Mother, Mother, what was that?
Hush, my darling! Only the cat.
(Patchy-scratchy, furry-purry,
Sneaky-peeky, cosy-dozy,
Prowly-yowly, sleepy-creepy,
Fighty-bitey, ever-so-mighty)
Out in the moony dark.

Trevor Millum

I think that with this poem I've managed to convey an important message without preaching or telling people what to think. At the same time, I'm pleased with both the story-telling approach – and the pattern of the poem. Sometimes it just feels as if all the aspects of writing have come together just right!

The Ballad of Unicorn Isle

Once upon a faraway time
Before the clocks had learned to chime
When every river spoke in rhyme
Once upon a time

Once within a distant land
Where mountains hadn't heard of man
Where dolphins played and bluebirds sang
Once within a land

Then and there in echoing light
Where gold was day and silver night
Lived unicorns of purest black and white
There in echoing light

One shining day in shimmering glade
The seer had come to speak, they said
An ancient one with eyes of jade
One shimmering shining day

'I saw the future far away –
Hearken friends to what I say!
I saw grey night and I saw grey day
In the future far away

I saw the pale two legged beast
Rise up from west, rise up from east
And slay our kind for fun and feast
The pale two-legged beast.

It hunted down the unicorn
It cut off head, it cut off horn
Or stole our foals as they were born
And caged the noble unicorn.'

Once upon a desperate hour
In the shadow of the great moonflower
They made a pact to use their power
Upon a desperate hour

So faded they from human sight
Though wild geese see them from their flight
And children dream of them at night
Invisible to human sight

Once within a faraway land
Where unicorns first heard of man
Where hotels rise and tourists tan
Once within a land…

Adrian Mitchell

To My Dog was written for Ella, who was my golden retriever until her death five years ago. I now have another golden retriever called Daisy the Dog of Peace – who is very well.

To My Dog

This gentle beast
This golden beast
laid her long chin
along my wrist

and my wrist
is branded
with her love
and trust

and the salt of my cheek
is hers to lick
so long as I
or she shall last

Tony Mitton

This is a favourite among my own poems partly because of its style, the way it manages to nudge ordinary speech into verse, which gives it a kind of easy, natural pace quite hard to get. And partly because it quietly insists that the world of imagination is as important as the world of everyday – that dream, fantasy and story make our lives richer, deeper and fuller.

Dreaming the Unicorn

I dreamed I saw the Unicorn
last night.
It rippled through the forest,
pearly white,
breathing a moonlit silence.

Its single horn
stood shining like a lance.
I saw it toss its head
and snort and prance
and paw the midnight air.
Its mane was like a mass
of silver hair.

My mind was wild, unclear.
I could not think or speak.
Above my head, I heard the branches creak
and then, from where I stood,
I watched it flicker off into the wood,
into the velvet space between the trees.

A sudden rush of rapid midnight breeze,
that felt both chill and deep,
awoke me from my sleep,
and there upon the pillow by my head
I found a strand of shining silver thread.

I kept that strand of mane,
I keep it, still,
inside a box upon my window sill.
And when the world hangs heavy
on my brain,
it helps me dream the Unicorn again.

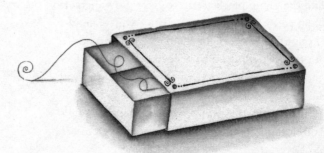

John Mole

I've always been fascinated by unsolved mysteries, and by poems which ask unanswerable questions. That's probably why I have a particular fondness for A Ghost Story. *Someone once suggested that poetry is a way of making familiar things strange and strange things familiar, and A Ghost Story is a poem in which I think I may have managed to do this.*

A Ghost Story

When you come home and it's raining
And there's nobody in
And the kettle's switched off but still steaming
And the biscuit tin
Is full of biscuits (your favourite kind)
And the beds have been made
And you look in the fridge and you find
Everything splendidly arrayed
For your best meal ever but when you call
Nobody answers and even the cat
(Who doesn't like rain) is not in the hall
Or the kitchen or upstairs or anywhere at all
And there's no message left on a table or the doormat
And the damp patch seems to have grown larger on the wall
Then you have to admit it at last – you're afraid
No not that they've gone and left you behind
But that you yourself have been delayed
And that somehow someone broke into your mind
Before you got home, and you'll have to begin
All over again, that you've woken from dreaming
And nothing has changed except nobody's in
(Not even the cat) and it's still raining.

Pat Moon

My gran may have been small, but she was a huge part of my life. She had no radio or television so I had to entertain myself: drawing, making dolls, reading — anything I could lay my hands on, and daydreaming friends, adventures and imaginary worlds. I didn't realise it then, but it was very good training for a writer. There's hardly a day goes by when I don't think about her.

Goodbye

My holidays were spent with Gran.
She was very small and very old.
In the evenings she'd tell stories
Of when she was even smaller,
And the saddest one she told
Was about her baby brother
Who they knew was going to die,
So all her family stood in line
To kiss him for the last time
And say goodbye.

She let me do things not allowed at home.
She cooked custard for breakfast
And brought it on a tray to me in bed.
She let me feed the pigeons on a window ledge.
But the best was the day when I said
How I'd like to make a bed in the bath.
So she tied up the taps,

Fetched blankets and sheets,
Lined it with pillows,
And I slept there for the week.

But I outgrew Gran.
As I grew taller she became the child.
My visits grew fewer.
Then one day when I called
She opened the door and smiled,
'Hello John. It is John, isn't it?'
'No, Gran, I'm the other one.'
(How could she mistake me for my brother?)

I was too busy growing up for childish games.
Too busy to drop by.
When I had the time,
Her time had run out.
It was too late to say goodbye.

Pamela Mordecai

There's a Jamaican proverb which goes: 'Jackass say de world no level'. I agree with jackass. A lot of the time it doesn't seem to be a very fair world. And one of the ways it can seem unfair is that adults, or 'big people', get to do things that children, or 'little people', can't do. I think that's why this poem is a favourite of mine. In the world of lizards and crickets and earthworms and rat bats, mothers and children do the same things: stick out their tongues, suck their teeth, play in the dirt, stay awake all night and sleep all day. And none of these is naughty – not for lizards and crickets and rat bats and earthworms, at any rate. Which is a lot more fair, isn't it?

If I Were

If I were a lizard
I'd lie around all day
And stick out my tongue
In a very naughty way.

And my mother couldn't tell me
It's a wicked thing to do
Since she would be a lizard
And she would do it too.

If I were a cricket
I'd hop around all day
And suck my teeth quite often
In a chirping sort of way.

And my mother couldn't tell me
It's a wicked thing to do
Since she would be a cricket
And she would do it too.

If I were a rat bat
Then I would sleep all day
And stay awake the livelong night
In a most upsetting way.

And my mother couldn't tell me
It's a wicked thing to do
Since she would be a rat bat
And she would do it too.

If I were an earthworm
I'd play in dirt all day
And drag my feet behind me
In a lazy sort of way.

And my mother couldn't tell me
It's a wicked thing to do,
Since she would be an earthworm
And she would do it too.

Michaela Morgan

At some time in my childhood I came across the poem The Tyger *by William Blake. It made an impression on me – and years later, when I read about the tiger losing its colour in captivity, the news story and Blake's poem collided in my mind and my poem was the result.*

Blake's Tyger – revisited

Tiger! Tiger! Turning white
In a cage just twice your height
Six paces left, six paces right,
A long slow day, a longer night.

Tiger! Tiger! Dreaming still
Of the scent? The chase? The kill?
And now? No need. No place. No scope.
No space. No point. No hope.

Tiger! Tiger! Paces. Paces.
Once he flashed through open spaces.
His world once echoed to his roars.
Now he's quiet. He stares. He snores.

An inch of sky glimpsed through the bars.
A puddle. Concrete. Smells of cars.
He sniffs the air. He slumps. He sighs.
And stares and stares through jaundiced eyes.

Brian Morse

I always like poems that mix serious ideas with comic images and when I feel I've managed this myself I'm really pleased. I also like the shape of Picnic on the Moon *and the way when I read it out, all the grown-ups in the room say, 'I bet you were thinking of the Clangers!'*

Picnic on the Moon

A picnic on the moon
  is a silent affair
    as absence of air
      is unconducive
        to serious conversation.

Sandwiches on the moon
  drift out of reach,
    hilarious the first time,
      funny the second.
        The pollution robot has been programmed
        to retrieve them.

Football on the moon
  is impossible.
    All ball-games are equally impossible,
      baseball, cricket, snooker.
        The okey-cokey is banned.

And when the party's over,
  then it's time to face
    the blue-and-green orb
      floating in the ethereal blackness, tug of Earth Mother
      lost for ever.

'Gather possessions.
  It is time to depart,'
    intones the robot-guide
      over the intercom.
        'The solar winds are turning.
          Gather possessions.'

After each departure
  the moon-mice come out to play.
    'Our grandparents saw the explosions,' they twitter.
    'They saw the explosions.
      What did they mean? What did they mean?'

Brian Moses

Turtles should be seen in the wild, not in captivity, and I feel that I have managed to say all that I wanted to say about the dignity of such creatures kept in inappropriate conditions.

The Lost Angels

In a fish tank in France
we discovered the lost angels,
fallen from heaven and floating now
on imaginary tides.
And all along the sides of the tank,
faces peered, leered at them,
laughing, pouting,
pointing, shouting,
while hung above their heads, a sign,
'Ne pas plonger les mains dans le bassin,'
Don't put your hands in the tank
– the turtles bite seriously.
And who can blame them,
these creatures with angels' wings,
drifting past like alien craft.
Who knows what signals they send
through an imitation ocean,
out of sight of sky,
out of touch with stars?
Dream on, lost angels,
then one day, one glorious day,
you'll flap your wings
and fly, again.

Judith Nicholls

I love to take a true story or series of facts and turn them into a poem — particularly where the subject is a mysterious one, as here. This poem was in fact started on a boat and I wanted to put across some of the sense of mystery and fear that the sea can give us.

Goodwin Sands

I have seen the pale gulls circle
against a restless sky;
I have heard the dark winds crying
as dusk-drawn clouds wheel by.

But the waiting waves still whisper
of shadowy ocean lands,
of twisting tides and of secrets
that lie beneath the Sands.

I have seen the wild weeds' tangle
and smelt the salted squall;
I have seen the moon rise from the seas,
and felt the long night's fall.

But whose are the voices that echo
from the shifting ocean lands,
that tell of secrets buried
beneath the drifting Sands?

For many sail the Goodwins
and some return to shore;
but others ride in the falling tide
and those are seen no more.

And voices rise from the waters
beneath a restless sky:
in the dying light of coming night
the long-lost sailors sigh;
from the watery lands of Goodwin Sands
I hear the sailors cry.

Grace Nichols

I've always loved trees and the mystery of the forests. Though written in England, the poem was inspired by the Guyana rainforests which I visited and which still have a big pull on my imagination.

For Forest

Forest could keep secrets
Forest could keep secrets

Forest tune in every day
to watersound and birdsound
Forest letting her hair down
to the teeming creeping of her forest-ground

But Forest don't broadcast her business
no Forest cover her business down
from sky and fast-eye sun
and when night come
and darkness wrap her like a gown
Forest is a bad dream woman

Forest dreaming about mountain
and when earth was young
Forest dreaming of the caress of gold
Forest rootsing with mysterious Eldorado

and when howler monkey
wake her up with howl
Forest just stretch and stir
to a new day of sound

but coming back to secrets
Forest could keep secrets
Forest could keep secrets

And we must keep Forest

Jack Ousbey

Shortly after my grand-daughter joined her secondary school she asked me if I could advise her about ways to improve her written work in English. I talked to her about the usual, dull practices like paragraphing, punctuation, variety in sentence forms and so on – and found it all so dry and mechanical I wrote her a poem instead. I like it: so did she.

Taking Hold

for Jenny

Make words work: make them tell the tale you want to tell.
Let them show who you are and how you feel: use words well.

Move words around: make them step out, march, advance.
Feel the pulse of them, the sway, the spring: make words dance.

Make words sound: hear them loud and clear, listen to their ring.
Hear them hum to each other, catch their tunes: make words sing.

Dig with words: turn up meanings, rake over, hoe.
Uncover buried stories, incantations: make words grow.

Polish words now: make them glint and glimmer, cast a spell.
Ready? Take hold then and dazzle us: wear words well.

Gareth Owen

I like the poem because it's simple and emotional. The phrase 'gathering in the day' refers to those odd moments when people stop what they're doing and gaze about them: thinking and not thinking; being there and at the same time not there. 'Gathering' also refers to bringing all these people I once knew together once more, so that we meet in the poem.

Gathering in the Days

I saw my grandad late last evening
On a hillside scything hay
Wiped his brow and gazed about him
Gathering in the day.

My grandmother beside the fireplace
Sleeps the afternoons away
Wakes and stirs the dying embers
Gathering in the day.

Heard screams and laughter from the orchard
Saw a boy and girl at play
Watched them turn their heads towards me
Gathering in the day.

And my mother at the window
On some long-forgotten May
Lifts her eyes and smiles upon us
Gathering in the day.

And all the people I remember
Stopped their lives and glanced my way
Shared the selfsame sun an instant
Gathering in the day.

Brian Patten

The teacher in the poem taught me when I was about twelve or thirteen years old. Writing the poem was a way of saying thank you to him for a lesson he never realised he was teaching me, and which I never knew I was being taught.

Geography Lesson

Our teacher told us one day he would leave
And sail across a warm blue sea
To places he had only known from maps,
And all his life had longed to be.

The house he lived in was narrow and grey
But in his mind's eye he could see
Sweet-scented jasmine clinging to the walls,
And green leaves burning on an orange tree.

He spoke of the lands he longed to visit,
Where it was never drab or cold.
I couldn't understand why he never left,
And shook off our school's stranglehold.

Then half-way through his final term
He took ill and never returned.
He never got to that place on the map
Where the green leaves of the orange tree burned.

The maps were redrawn on the classroom wall;
His name forgotten, he faded away.
But a lesson he never knew he taught
Is with me to this day.

I travel to where the green leaves burn,
To where the ocean's glass-clear and blue,
To places my teacher taught me to love –
And which he never knew.

Andrew Fusek Peters

This poem sums up all my feelings about the countryside where I live and my favourite time of year. This river (the Onny in Shropshire) is a magical place full of tiny trout, distant views and clean water. A fitting subject for a poem.

The Pool

We wade through corn like tigers on fire,
And run the obstacle course of barbed wire,
To follow the stream in a winding dream,
Until in a corner, scooped like ice cream,
Under the alders, a hidden pool,
I trail my fingers in the willowy cool.
The grass is bullied and nettles beaten,
Blankets laid for food to be eaten
We leap like salmon one, two, three,
Divebombers of this inland sea,
Hit the water, bodies froze,
Suddenly trout are tickling toes,
The oak is a mast in the ship of shade
Cows drift through the grassy glade
Heads bent like old men reading the news,
As beyond, the hills hold distant views
Under the beaming fat lady sun,
Witch of warmth, conjuring fun,
Until she grows tired and a little bit low,

And daylight packs up, ready to go!
Oh why can't summer last forever,
And why can't we take home this river?
In twilight we stumble through itchy corn,
Get caught on barbed wire with trousers torn,
Sleepily falling into cars
To carry us home under rippling stars.

Gervase Phinn

I met a small boy in a school in the Yorkshire Dales who told me sadly he was 'not much good at anything really'. His writing was spidery and untidy and his spelling very poor. He might not have been too good at writing but my goodness he was an expert at things I knew nothing about. I usually write funny poems but was inspired to write something a little more thoughtful, perhaps with a message that we are all different, that there is always someone who is better at one thing or another and that we all have special talents.

A Child of the Dales

From the classroom window rolled the great expanse of the
  Dale.
The sad child in the corner stared out like a rabbit in a trap.
'He has special needs,' explained the teacher, in a hushed,
  maternal voice.
'Real problems with his reading, and his number work is
  weak.
Spelling non-existent, writing poor. He rarely speaks.
He's one of the less able in the school.'

The lad could not describe the beauty that surrounded him:
The soft green dale and craggy hills.
He could not spell the names
Of those mysterious places which he knew so well.
But he could tickle a trout, ride a horse,
Repair a fence and dig a dyke,
Drive a tractor, plough a field,
Milk a cow and lamb a ewe,
Name a bird with a faded feather
Smell the seasons and predict the weather,
Yes, that less able child could do all those things.

Joan Poulson

Song About a Drummer is a poem that arrived on a sparkly cloud and slipped into my computer: a gift. I love the rhythm and unusual language of it. It isn't easy to read because it demands a good pace — but it's great fun! Audiences of all ages seem to enjoy hearing it as much as I delight in reading it.

Song About a Drummer

O my mammy sang a song
about a drummer down the cellar
but this green-eyed drummer
was no ordinary feller –
he'd a purple chimney hat,
a crazy, steeleye band,
wore yellow high-heeled boots,
carried magic in his hand…

magic in the drumsticks
dub-a-dub, beat,
frizzle-up your furlylocks
rap-tap through your feet…

and the purple chimney hat
rang with the voice of the drum
and the crazy, steeleye band
sang calypsos to the sun.

142

In his yellow high-heeled boots
the drummer leaped from the cellar
and my mammy led him dancing
where the waves crash and bellow

there they rap-tap whirled
till the moon grew pale
saw them twirl into the sun-rise
on a gentian-backed whale
and my silver-haired mammy
kept the secret of the cellar
never telling
where the drummer could be found...

magic in the drumsticks
dub-a-dub, beat,
frizzle-up your furlylocks
rap-tap through your feet.

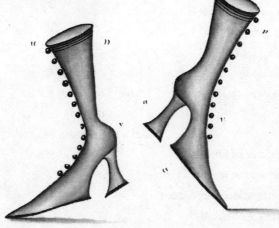

John Rice

Scottish poets like myself often have a go at writing simple little song-like poems in the Scots/Irish traditional style. Dazzledance has become one of my most popular poems and has been set to music and recorded by the Irish singer Padraigin Ni Uallachain. One of the things I tried to do in Dazzledance was to mention Story, Music, Song and Dance – four of the most important art forms in Scottish tradition – within the framework of a poem.

Dazzledance

I have an eye of silver,
I have an eye of gold,
I have a tongue of reed-grass
and a story to be told.

I have a hand of metal,
I have a hand of clay,
I have two arms of granite
and a song for every day.

I have a foot of damson,
I have a foot of corn,
I have two legs of leaf-stalk
and a dance for every morn.

I have a dream of water,
I have a dream of snow,
I have a thought of wildfire
and a harp-string long and low.

I have an eye of silver,
I have an eye of gold,
I have a tongue of reed-grass
and a story to be told.

Cynthia Rider

I chose this poem because it is about one of my favourite places, the Dolgoch Falls in Wales. These waterfalls have a mystery and magic all of their own and writing about them was a good way of holding on to some of that magic.

Waterfall
(acrostic)

Water, white as a veil,
Arches across rocks, falls,
Tosses in turbulent torrents,
Excites, enchants, enthrals.
Rushing and racing it roars, pours,
Furious and fast. Fantastic it spills.
Amazingly splintered it thrills.
Leaps, light-sparkling and lithe.
Lands and lingers in limpid, lace-edged pools.

Michael Rosen

*I wondered what it would be like to be a baby zooming along in a
buggy. Then I thought you'd probably feel like some king of the road
and the best way to boast in a poem these days seems to be a rap…
then it just boasted its way on to the page. That's why I like it.*

Boogy Woogy Buggy

I glide as I ride
in my boogy woogy buggy
take the corners wide
just see me drive
I'm an easy speedy baby
doing the baby buggy jive.

I'm in and out the shops
I'm the one that never stops
I'm the one that feels
the beat of the wheels
all that air
in my hair
I streak down the street
between the feet that I meet.

No one can catch
my boogy woogy buggy
no one's got the pace
I rule this place.

I'm a baby who knows
I'm a baby who goes, baby, *goes.*

Coral Rumble

I don't think You're Dead *is my best poem but it's probably my favourite. It has 'broken the ice' for me wherever I've performed it, and draws the audience in with its irresistible refrain. Like an old friend, it can always be trusted.*

You're Dead

If you copy from a friend
You're dead,
If you give the truth a bend
You're dead,
If you run instead of walk
Or shout instead of talk
You're dead,
You're dead;

If you forget your pencil case
You're dead,
If you make a funny face
You're dead,
If your pages are all blotchy
Your teacher will go potty
You're dead,
You're dead;

If you walk over the grass
You're dead,
If you pick your nose in class
You're dead,
If your reading book gets lost
You'll have to pay the cost
You're dead,
You're dead;

If you're talking at the back
You're dead,
If your fingernails are black
You're dead,
If you're late in your arriving
Not much chance of you
surviving
You're dead,
You're dead;

If you fail the tables test
You're dead,
If you take a little rest
You're dead,
If your games kit's being washed
Or your topic's sort of squashed
You're dead,
You're dead;

If you jump the dinner queue
You're dead,
If your name's scratched on the loo
You're dead,
If your homework is in late
Then you'll have to meet your fate
You're dead,
You're dead;

If you're sent to see the head
You're dead,
If his face gets kind of red
You're dead,
If he reaches for the phone
And makes contact with your home
YOU'RE DEAD!

Vernon Scannell

I wrote this – or a version of this – poem while I was still at school, about fourteen years old, so I probably have a sentimental attachment to it. But that's not the only reason for choosing it. I have found that children of all ages do respond to and enjoy more serious, even melancholy poems such as this.

The Day That Summer Died

From all around the mourners came
The day that Summer died,
From hill and valley, field and wood
And lane and mountainside.

They did not come in funeral black
But every mourner chose
Gorgeous colours or soft shades
Of russet, yellow, rose.

Horse chestnut, oak and sycamore
Wore robes of gold and red;
The rowan sported scarlet beads;
No bitter tears were shed.

Although at dusk the mourners heard,
As a small wind softly sighed,
A touch of sadness in the air
The day that Summer died.

Fred Sedgwick

I like this poem because I am very fond of my god-daughter, for whom it was written; because I like using strict forms (this is a kyrielle); because it has been set to music by the composer Sheena Billet and because I like poems with my ginger tom Stanley in them (see line seven). Also, I like it because the poem is about my faith, which I usually find difficult to write about.

Lord of All Gardens
(kyrielle)
for Rebecca Moore on the occasion of her first communion, 10 June 2001

The garden's soaked in sunlight where,
Marooned in my mortality,
I stand and murmur common prayer:
Lord of all gardens, pray for me.

Mysteriously float the scents
Of herb and flower, grass and tree.
The cat hunts slyly by the fence.
Lord of all gardens, pray for me.

Where the sky above me stands
Clouds' silent music's drifting free.
My mind is still. So are my hands.
Lord of all gardens, pray for me.

With the wide world, or all alone;
Whether in air, on land or sea,
My heart won't turn to sand or stone –
Lord of all gardens, pray for me.

Norman Silver

I like the way the poem isn't really complimentary about the mother until the last line, when it becomes clear that the verses are meant affectionately. Sometimes it's hard to tell someone that you love them.

＞

A Card for Mother's Day

You're cuddlier than a nettle,
kinder than a great white shark,
jollier than a graveyard
at midnight in the dark,

calmer than a thunderstorm,
neater than sloshy mud,
more elegant than a hippo
or a cow that's chewing cud,

lovelier than a potato,
gentler than an avalanche,
more charming than a squawking crow
squatting on its branch,

livelier than a bathroom sponge,
warmer than Arctic ice,
more generous than a teaspoon
with a single grain of rice,

softer than a ball and chain,
wiser than a wooden plank,
because today is Mother's Day
it's you I have to thank

for everything you've done for me,
for keeping me in your clutch,
you're sweeter than lime pickle
and I love you very much.

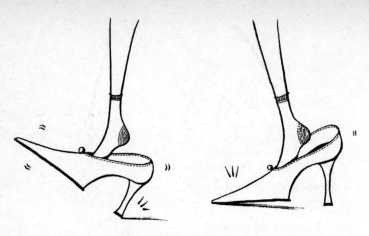

Matt Simpson

*This poem simply started with a funny name (Melanie Wilberforce)
but ended up being about a real event I could hear happening as I
was writing. Melanie (not her real name) is grown-up now and
Charlie (not his real name) is at comprehensive school and mad on
football. The poem wants to be kind and hold time back a bit before
something awful happens.*

One Spring Day

Melanie, Melanie Wilberforce
Knows just how it feels
To clatter on the garden path
In her mam's high heels.

Baby brother, Charlie,
Is snoozing in his pram
Underneath the washing line
Like a little lamb.

Clatter, clatter, crunch, crunch,
Those spiky heels go,
Crunch, scrape, clatter, clack…
Little does she know

That Charlie's going to wake and bawl
Any minute now
And mum is going to dash outside
And make poor Melanie howl.

But until that awful moment comes
Let little Charlie snooze
And Melanie scrape the concrete
In her mam's best shoes.

This world is full of troubles,
So let the baby snore
And Melanie go a-clattering
Half a minute more.

Roger Stevens

*Whenever I read this poem in schools teachers always say to me –
'You used to be a teacher, didn't you?' I say, 'Yes, how did you
know?' And they say, 'Because that poem is exactly right.' Teachers
DO have that secret, hidden plug.*

What Teacher Does at Night

When the chalk dust settles
And the children have gone home
And a kind of empty quietness fills the room
The teacher gives a gentle tug
To her hidden plastic plug
And slowly she deflates, like a balloon

Matthew Sweeney

I like reading this poem to audiences and it's one children seem to really relish. And I enjoy the fact that a nasty poem like that has such a sweet title, as if it's going to be a nice poem, maybe even a love poem, so people read it with that expectation and get ambushed by the nastiness at the end.

Honey

The bee buzzed over the honey pot
left open on the table.
'That's mine,' he thought, 'not theirs!
They're as bad as grizzly bears.
I'm going to steal it back if I'm able.'

He hovered and buzzed and dipped
below the rim of the pot
till he could sniff and smell his fill.
It was foreign honey, but still.
Home in the hive there wasn't a lot.

He buzzed in a figure-of-eight
and dodged the sticky spoon.
He flew up and landed on the rim.
How would he get the honey home?
He'd better hurry. They'd be back soon.

Should he go to the hive for help?
Bring a swarm back
to carry each sweet drop at once,
with a dozen bees hanging loose
to guard in case of attack?

He buzzed down to the honey again.
He'd better taste it first.
Who knew what had been done with it?
Boiled, or stuff mixed in with it?
They were known to do their worst.

He landed gently on the meniscus.
He dipped a claw inside
and brought a sticky drop to his mouth.
Six out of ten, he'd tasted worse.
It was time he headed for the hive.

But when he flapped his papery wings
he saw he was stuck there.
He flapped so hard he began to hum.
He telepathized the Queen to come
but he stayed stuck there

till a boy came in and found him,
and pulled his wings off
and squeezed him till he was dead
then spread him, with honey, on bread –
over half a French loaf

which the boy gave to his sister
as they sat down to tea,
and the boy crumbled a bee wing
while the girl swallowed a bee sting.
'Mmn,' she said. 'Wonderful honey!'

Marian Swinger

I meant this to be a nonsense poem but it turned out quite sensible after all. You can get bogged down in the mundane and never see the things that matter.

The Picnic

They biked to the edge of the world one day
where the sea tumbled over the brink,
took out some cans and a couple of cups
and poured themselves something to drink.
They gazed at the waters cascading
in a foaming and terrible wall
and murmured (while spreading a cloth out)
that the world must be flat after all.

They brought out some ketchup and marmite
as a phoenix erupted in flames
and they ate cheese baguettes spread with pickle
before they got up for a game.
A unicorn nibbled their cupcakes
as they dribbled a football around
swatting at minuscule dragons
which fluttered in swarms from the ground.
As the sun set in fiery glory
and the sea put it out with a hiss,
they cleared up their rubbish and yawning,
tossed it into the abyss.
The night sky was blazing with starlight
as the pair of them cycled away.
They arrived home at three in the morning
and were late in for work the next day.

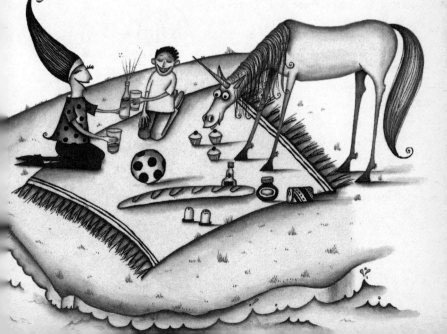

Nick Toczek

The Meat Boutique was a wonderfully-named butcher's shop in Bradford. Perhaps because I'm a vegetarian, I began to dream up this bizarre idea of it selling clothes (as ordinary boutiques do) but made out of meat. From this came a grotesque imaginary world of meat. So, The Meat Boutique's a favourite poem because it's wacky and fun to perform.

The Meat Boutique

With the chic, freak clique from the Meat Boutique
you wake in bacon, shave in gravy,
take a wash in a warm goulash,
hit the street in a suit of meat
and knock 'em flat, knock 'em flat,
knock 'em flat in your pork-pie hat.

Then…
Wham! Bam!
Beef 'n' lamb.
Mutton your button
'n' stew your shoe.

Advertisement:
'Feel fresh as flesh with twice the charm.
Try gammon roll-on underarm!'

God damn
veal 'n' ham!
Walk 'n' talk
as suave as pork.

Advertisement:
'Don't waste yourself, baste yourself!
Life is easy, bright 'n' breezy
when you make your skin go greasy.
Don't be a drip in dripping.
Don't be a prat in fat.
It's lard, lard for the lad who's hard.
If it ain't lard, it's lah-di-dah!'

So…
Slam! Blam!
Brawn 'n' spam.
Sirloin steak 'n'
streaky bacon.

Wham! Bam!
Beef 'n' lamb.
Mutton your button
'n' stew your shoe.

God damn
veal 'n' ham!
Walk 'n' talk
as suave as pork…

…KAZAM!
Unique, sleek, at their peak,
they're the chic, freak clique,
the chic, freak clique,
the chic, freak clique from the Meat Boutique
AH-HAAAAAH!

Angela Topping

This poem is my favourite because I love the way it mixes the real with the fairytale. The child who is speaking in the poem is trying to get the adult to notice the amazing thing she has seen. Adults are too often busy being responsible to notice things like a witch calmly shopping. I enjoyed making up all the horrible things a witch would buy and it is always good when rhymes work out, as they are hard to do.

Witch in the Supermarket

There's a witch in the supermarket over there
After Fowler's treacle for her flyaway hair,
Buying up nail-varnish – black or green?
Rooting in the freezer for toad ice-cream!

There's a witch in the supermarket next row on
Asking where the Tinned Bats' Ears have gone,
Mutters, 'Why do they always change things round?
Mouse Tails and Rats' Tongues can't be found!'

There's a witch in the supermarket down that aisle
Searching for something to blacken her smile,
She's a trolley full of tins for her witch's cat
Who simply swears by Bit-O-Bat.

Times are difficult and Bovril has to do
Instead of newt's blood for a tasty stew;
Sun-dried bluebottles crunchy and sweet,
Desiccated spiders for a Hallowe'en treat.

There's a witch in the supermarket at the till
Scribbling her cheque with a grey goose quill!
There's a witch at the checkout, look, mum, quick!
Piling up her shopping on a big broomstick!

Steve Turner

I had set myself the task of telling a story in the shortest poem possible and was waiting for my subject to arrive. It was while sitting outside a café in Portugal that the events in this poem took place and provided me with my story. It's very satisfying to complete a technical challenge that you've set yourself and I liked the word play which helped hold the poem together.

The Death of a Fly

Fly see saucer
Fly fly down
Me see fly fly
Fly walk 'round.

Fly take big sip
Me take spoon
Fly look wrong way
Spoon go boom.

Cup go wobble
Tea go splat
Fly get big fright
Fly get flat.

Fly not fly now
Fly not sip
Fly just flied on
Final trip.

Kaye Umansky

This is a poem I wrote years ago when I was a brand new, just published author. I like it because it reads aloud well and is totally daft.

My Father is a Werewolf

My father is a werewolf,
Right now he's busy moulting.
He leaves his hairs on stairs and chairs,
It's really quite revolting.
And if my friends make comments
(For some of them are faddy)
I tell them it's the cat or dog.
I never say it's Daddy.

Barrie Wade

I like puzzles and I think a poem should not give up all its meaning at once. I also think poems should be read aloud and that's the way to solve this one.

Code Shoulder

'L.O.' Z. I.

'L.O.' Z. U.

'R. U. O. K?' I. Z.

'I. B. O. K,' U. Z.

'I. 1. 2. C. U.' Z. I.

'Y?' Z. U.

'U. R. D. 1. 4. I.' I. Z.

'O. I!' U. Z.

'U. R. A. D.R.' Z. I.

'O!' Z. U.

'I. B. D. 1. 4. U. 2.' I. Z.

'N.E. I.D.R. Y?' U. Z.

'I. B. A. B.U.T. 4. N.E.1. 2. C.' Z. I

'I. 8. U.' Z. U.

'O. D.R!' Z. I.

Celia Warren

I love languages. I also enjoy inventing words and imaginary people and places. I like writing letters, too. This poem involves all those things. Whenever I read it to children they can always translate all the Sprong words, so then I enjoy pretending that they come from the Planet Sprong. Maybe they do?

Dear Alien

I newly learn your Earth-speak –
forgive if I get it wrong.
When I don't know the Earth-word
I shall have to write in *Sprong*.

Sorry to start 'Dear Alien',
but now our planets are twinned,
I hope as we get to know each other
we shall want to write 'Dear *fribble*'.

I am thirty-two, in Sprong-years;
in Earth-years, I'd be eight.
My mum's one-hundred-and-twenty today
so we're going to celebrate.

She's invited us all to a *poggle*,
and baked a birthday-cake,
with a hundred and twenty *clabbits* on top.
(Is my Earth-speak without mistake?)

Me, please, to tell what I wrong get,
my lovely new pen-*fribble*.
I want to learn all about the Earth.
Write and tell me all your *gribble*.

I shall now tell you what I look like:
My hair is short and red
on my arms and legs, and greenish-*grump*
and curly on my head.

My *ecklings* are blue and yellow,
with the middle one black and white.
I'm told that Earthlings have only two –
can you really see all right?

I have a brother and sister,
and a lovely pet *splink* called 'Bloggs'.
Is it true you have pets with four legs and a tail?
What do you call them – droggs?

Please write back soon, dear Earthling,
don't keep me waiting long –
and remember to tell me your Earth-words
that, today, I've written in *Sprong*.

Colin West

Toboggan is my favourite poem because it's short and good fun. I like the sound of all those b's and g's when it's recited quite fast — although the rhythm reminds me more of a train than a toboggan!

Toboggan

To begin to toboggan, first buy a toboggan,
But don't buy too big a toboggan.
(A too big a toboggan is not a toboggan
To buy to begin to toboggan.)

David Whitehead

I like this poem because it has a bouncy rhythm like a wallaby. It also asks the question can you ever be anyone but yourself?

I Wannabe a Wallaby

I wannabe a wallaby,
A wallaby that's true.
Don't wannabe a possum
A koala or a roo.

I wannago hop hopping
Anywhere I please.
Hopping without stopping
Through eucalyptus trees.

A wallaby, a wallaby
Is what I wannabe.
I'd swap my life to be one,
But a problem – I can see;

If I'm gonna be a wallaby
I shall have to go and see
If I can find a wallaby,
A very friendly wallaby,
Who would really, really, really…

Wannabe… ME!

Ian Whybrow

My friend Dave Mander and I loved going on trains when we were boys. We loved the noise of them, the tunes they played and the way they heaved smoke and sparks. Every morning we arrived at our school, St Saviours, Westgate on Sea, our hair and clothes smelling like coal-furnaces because it was our ritual to wait on the footbridge until the London express pulled out of the station and blasted a smothering cloud of smoke up through the boards. Most people ran squealing but not us; this was our daily baptism, our fountain of holy smoke, our small consolation for not being on board and away down the line.

The Last Steam Train to Margate
for Allan Rothwell

Gossssh
I wisssh
I were a busss
It's muccch less work
And muccch less fuss
I ssshould like that
I ssschould like that
I SSSSCHOULD like that
I ssshould like that
De-deedle-dee
De-diddle-dum
Just look at me
'Cause here I come
Faster and faster

Tickerty-boo, what'll I do?
Tearing along, terribly fast
Singing a song, sounding a blast
Whoo, whoo! Out of the way
Goodness me, I can't delay!
You can relax, I have to run
Follow the tracks into the sun
Pain in my back, aches in my joints
Tickerty-tack, here are the points
Diddly-dee, diddly dee
Diddly WIDDLY diddly dee!
Far to go? Not very far.
Little black tunnel
(Tickerty WHAAAH!)
Look over there. What can it be?
Lucky old you, clever old me

Come every day, singing a song
Down to the seaside. Let's have a cheer.
Oh, what a train-ride. We're nearly there,
We're nearly there, we're nearly there, we're nearly there
And now I'd better slow right down
In half a mile we reach the town
And then you take your buckets and spades
And dig the sand and watch the parades
And sing and paddle and splash in the sea
And have ice cream and jelly for tea
And Coca Cola, orange squassssh
And ginger beer, hooray we're here
But gosssh I'm tired
Oh gosssh I'm tired
Oh gosssh I'm tired
Hohhh
GOSSSSSSSSSSSSSSSSHHHHHHHHHHHHHHH

Benjamin Zephaniah

I think animals ought to have a voice, and if I can lend my voice creatively and in a nice way to animals, then I do. I love the storytelling and how the worms and different animals, such as snakes, are saying: Look, we matter too.

We People Too

I have dreams of summer days
Of running freely on the lawn
I luv a lazy Sunday morn
Like many others do.
I luv my family always
I luv clear water in a stream
Oh yes I cry and yes I dream
We dogs are people too.

When I have time I luv sightseeing
You may not want to see my face
But you and me must share a space
Like many others do.
Please think of me, dear human being,
It seems that I'm always in need
I have a family to feed
We mice are people too.

They say we're really dangerous
But we too like to feel and touch
And we like music very much
Like many others do.
Most of us are not poisonous
I have a little lovely face
I move around with style and grace
We snakes are people too.

And I, dear folk, am small and great
My friends call me the mighty Bruce
I luv to drink pure orange juice
Like many others do.
I hope you all appreciate
We give you all a helping hand
When me and my friends turn the land
We worms are people too.

I don't mind if you stand and stare
But know that I have luv no end
And my young ones I will defend
Like many others do.
When you see me in the air
Remember that I know the worth
Of all us who share the earth
We birds are people too.

I need fresh air and exercise
I need to safely cross the road,
I carry such a heavy load
Like many others do.
Don't only judge me by my size
Ask any veterinarian
I'm just a vegetarian
We cows are people too.

Water runs straight off my smooth back
And I hold my head high with pride
I like my children at my side
Like many others do.
I don't care if you're white or black
If you like land or air or sea
I want to see more unity
We ducks are people too.

I think living is so cool
And what I really like the most
Is kiss chase and I luv brown toast
Like many others do.
I hang around in a big school
I only need a little sleep
I like thinking really deep
We fish are people too.

I luv the cows I love the trees
And I would rather you not smoke
For if you smoke then I would choke
Like many others do.
I beg you do not squash me please
I do not want to cause you harm
I simply want you to stay calm
We flies are people too.

My name is Thomas Tippy Tops
Billy is not my name
I've learnt to live with fame
Like many others do.
I once was on Top of the Pops
On TV I sang loud
My parents were so proud
We goats are people too.

I luv to walk among the fern
I'm thankful for each night and day
I really luv to holiday
Like many others do.
I've read the books and my concern
Is why do we always look bad?
My friends don't think I'm raving mad
We wolves are people too.

A lovely garden makes me smile
A good joke makes me croak
One day I want to own a boat
Like many others do.
I'd luv to see the river Nile
I'd luv my own sandcastle
I really want to travel
We frogs are people too.

Please do not call me horrid names
Think of me as a brother
I'm quite nice you'll discover
Like many others do.
If you're my friend then call me James
I'll be your friend for ever more
I'll be the one that you adore
We pigs are people too.

We really need this planet
And we want you to be aware
We just don't have one spare
Not any of us do.

We dogs, we goats
We mice, we snakes
Even we worms
Are really great,
We birds, we cows
We ducks, we frogs
Are just trying to do our jobs
We wolves, we fish
We pigs, we flies
Could really open up your eyes
And all we want to say to you
Is that
We all are people too.

Ann Ziety

I'm fond of this poem because I've always had a soft spot for the underdog, the person who doesn't fit, the person everybody laughs at. The language is very alive — you can almost taste, smell and feel the words, which I think makes poor old Scrunge even more revolting.

At the Bottom

Scrunge Shrimpkin
at the bottom of the ooze
lived on globularis
swollen with mud
pumped up with sloop
and sloppy despicables
        but I loved him

Scrunge Shrimpkin
pottled around on the river's slimy mattress
wallowed in ancient nasties
gorged his shovel-mouth with shrivelled death
and snored
like a motorbike throbbing over a cattle-grid
        but I loved him none-the-less

he lummered over the encrusted scum
like a scaly sea-adder, frothy-mouthed
full of gastric fumes and fish oil
fashioned in filth
sieving seaweed seed pods through his gut
knitting grey hummus out of algae-smothered crisp packets
wrinkled in the sog
Scrunge Shrimpkin pissed on his own foot
      but I loved him

      and it wasn't easy

'Hey Scrunge!' the kids used to shout
'He's got odd socks on!'
and Scrunge would slither back
in deep
down
faster than falling
and fasten his bulk onto the very bottom bog
cover his ugly ears with sog-clods
fiddle with his tubes
blow out little spores of sadness
and bellow into the black

vagabond abalones nibbled at his slack skin
the colour of lard
and demon dribblers raked his back
cooked in the bubbling squishy
Scrunge Shrimpkin
was al dente
but in the middle of a heave
he blew great gobbers of poison
at the skinny pilchards
and squirmed into the slush
safe
and
sound

Scrunge Shrimpkin
made a hole
in the glaucous, soft hills
combed his tendrils tickled with daphnia
snored
like a manatee with adenoids
and was buried at the bottom of the world

      but I loved him

Index of Titles and First Lines

⤜ Acknowledgements ⤛

The publishers gratefully acknowledge the following for permission to reproduce
copyright material in this anthology.

John Agard: 'from Points of View With Professor Peekaboo', first published in *Points of View With Professor Peekaboo* (Random House Children's Books) copyright © John Agard 2000. **Allan Ahlberg**: 'Lost', from *Please Mrs Butler* by Allan Ahlberg (Kestrel, 1983) copyright © Allan Ahlberg 1983. **Jez Alborough**: 'The Assembly Cough' copyright © Jez Alborough 2002, published for the first time in this edition by permission of the author. **Moira Andrew**: 'Letter from Egypt' copyright © Moira Andrew, first published in *A Christmas Stocking* edited by Wes Magee (Cassell, 1988). **Leo Aylen**: 'Greedy Green River', first published in *Big World, Little World* edited by Sue Stewart (Nelson Thornes, 1992) copyright © Leo Aylen. **Gerard Benson**: 'River Song', first published in *Evidence of Elephants, Poems by Gerard Benson* (Viking, 1995), by permission of the author. **James Berry**: 'Draped With Water', published for the first time in this edition by permission of the author. **Malorie Blackman**: 'I've Done It Again!' is taken from her book *Pig-Heart Boy* (Doubleday/Corgi – Transworld Publishers). **Valerie Bloom**: 'De', first published in *Let Me Touch The Sky* by Valerie Bloom (Macmillan Children's Books) reproduced by permission of the author. **Tony Bradman**: 'The Thing', reproduced by permission of The Agency (London) Ltd. Tony Bradman © 2000. First published in *Here Come the Heebie Jeebies* by Hodder Children's Books. **Sandy Brownjohn**: 'Nine Lives', from *Both Sides of the Catflap* (Hodder Children's Books, 1996). **James Carter**: 'The Dark', from *Cars, Stars, Electric Guitars* © 2002 James Carter. Reproduced by permission of the publisher, Walker Books Ltd., London. **Charles Causley**: 'By St Thomas Water', first published in *Collected Poems for Children* by Charles Causley (Macmillan Children's Books, 1996). **Faustin Charles**: 'Once Upon an Animal', copyright © Faustin Charles and Bloomsbury Children's Books Ltd., 1998. **Debjani Chatterjee**: 'Aching Bones', first published in *Animal Antics*, (Pennine Pens, 2000), by permission of the author. **Gillian Clarke**: 'Horse of the Sea', first published in *The Animal Wall and other poems* (Pont Books, 1999) **John Coldwell**: 'The Cupboard on the Landing', first published in *The Slack-Jawed Camel* (Stride, 1992). **Paul Cookson**: 'Let No-one Steal Your Dreams' first published in *Let No-one Steal Your Dreams* (A Twist In The Tail, 1994). **Wendy Cope**: 'Sensible-Bensible', first published in 1994 and reproduced by permission of the author. **Pie Corbett**: 'City Jungle', first published in *Rice, Pie & Moses* (Macmillan, 1995) copyright © Pie Corbett. **John Cotton**: 'Oscar the Dog', first published in *Oscar the Dog and Friends* (Longmans, 1994). **Sue Cowling**: 'Leaves', first published in *What is a Kumquat?* (Faber and Faber, 1991). **Kevin Crossley-Holland**: 'The Desert Singer', reproduced by permission of the author. **John Cunliffe**: 'If You Come to Our House', first published in *Fizzy Whizzy Poetry Book* (Scholastic). **Jan Dean**: 'Sports Day', first published in *Nearly Thirteen* by Jan Dean (Blackie, 1995). **Peter Dixon**: 'Biento', published for the first time in this edition by permission of the author. **Berlie Doherty**: 'Badger', first published in *Casting a Spell* compiled by Angela Huth (Orchard Books, 1991). **Gina Douthwaite**: 'Rhino', first published in *Wacky Wild Animals* (Macmillan Children's Books, 2000) copyright © Gina Douthwaite. **Carol Ann Duffy**: 'The Cord', copyright © Carol Ann Duffy. **Michael Dugan**: 'Sound Advice', copyright © Michael Dugan. **Helen Dunmore**: 'Smiles Like Roses', from *Snollygoster* by Helen Dunmore copyright © Helen Dunmore, 2001 first published by Scholastic Children's Books, 2001, reproduced by permission of Scholastic Ltd. **Richard Edwards**: 'The Glove and the Guitar', reproduced by permission of the author. **Max Fatchen**: 'Windy Work', from *A Paddock of Poems* (Omnibus/Puffin Australia, 1987). **Eric Finney**: 'Learning the Flowers', first published in *Scholastic Collections: Poetry* compiled by Wes Magee (Scholastic, 1992) copyright © Eric Finney. **John Foster**: 'It Isn't Right To Fight', copyright © 1995 John Foster from *Standing on the Sidelines* (Oxford University Press). **Pam Gidney**: 'Horrible Henry', first published in *Never Play Snap with a Shark* edited by John Foster (Macmillan Children's Books, 2001). **Mick Gowar**: 'Boots', reproduced by kind permission of the author. **David Harmer**: 'The Prime Minister is Ten Today', first published in *The Very Best of David Harmer* (Macmillan Children's Books, 2001). **Michael Harrison**: 'Diary', first published in *Junk Mail* (Oxford University Press, 1993). **Anne Harvey**: 'Miss Simpkins', first published in *The Twenty-first Guildhall Anthology*, 1993. Copyright © Anne Harvey. **John Hegley**: 'Uncle and Auntie', André Deutsch, 1990. **Stewart Henderson**: 'Sometimes', first published in the collection: *Who Left Grandad at the Chipshop?* by Stuart Henderson (Lion Books: hardback 2000, paperback 2001). **Diana Hendry**: 'The Cullen Skink', first published in *Borderers* (Peterloo Poets, 2001). **Russell Hoban**: 'The Ghost Horse of Chingis Khan', first published in *The Last of the Wallendas* (Hodder Children's Books). **Libby Houston**: 'The Old Woman and the Sandwiches', first published in *All Change* (Oxford University Press, 1993) © Libby Houston. **Robert Hull**: 'Dear Mrs James', published for the first time in this edition. **Jenny Joseph**: 'The Hunter Evades the Guardians', first published in *All the Things I See* by Jenny Joseph (Macmillan Children's Books, 2000). **Michael Jubb**: 'School is Closed Today Because…', first published in *Excuses Excuses* (Oxford University Press, 1997) copyright © Michael Jubb. **Jackie Kay**: 'Brendon Gallacher', first published in *Two's Company* (Blackie, 1991). Currently published by Puffin Books. **Daphne Kitching**: 'Growing Up', first published in *As Long as There are Trees* (Kingston Press, 2001). **John Kitching**: 'Haiku Year', published for the first time in this edition, by permission of the author. **Tony Langham**: 'Linguist', published here for the first time by permission of the author. **Dennis Lee**: 'The Question', copyright © Dennis Lee. **Patricia Leighton**: 'Rock Pool Rock', first published in *Ridiculous Rhymes* picked by John Foster (Collins Children's Books, 2001). **J. Patrick Lewis**: 'Stories', copyright © 1991 by J. Patrick Lewis. **John Lyons**: 'Chickichong', first published in *a Caribbean Dozen* edited by John Agard and Grace Nichols (Walker Books, 1996). **Lindsay MacRae**: 'The Babysitter', first published in *How to Avoid Kissing Your Parents in Public* (Puffin, 2000). **Roger McGough**: 'The Man Who Steals Dreams', copyright © Roger McGough. Reprinted by